CW00506456

For Maggie
with many thanks
for your
lovely paintings

Nigel Sitwell

Galápagos

**GUÍA DE LOS ANIMALES Y LAS PLANTAS
EN ESPAÑOL**

**A GUIDE TO THE ANIMALS AND PLANTS
IN ENGLISH**

**EIN TIER-UND PFLANZENFÜHRER
AUF DEUTSCH**

Nigel Sitwell

❙ Ilustraciones ❙ Illustrations by ❙ Illustrationen von
**Sarah Darwin, Thalia Grant, Denys Ovenden,
Maggie Raynor, Mary Ellen Taylor**

Wilmot Books

First published in 2011 by Wilmot Books, an imprint of Ocean Explorer Maps, Lakeside House, Quarry Lane, Chichester, PO19 8NY, England

Text copyright © 2011 by Nigel Sitwell

Illustrations copyright © 2011 by Sarah Darwin, Thalia Grant, Denys Ovenden, Maggie Raynor, and Mary Ellen Taylor respectively

A CIP catalogue record for this book is available from the British Library.

ISBN 978-0-9543717-8-4

For DWS

El color **rojo** corresponde al texto en español.

In this book **blue** indicates text in English.

In diesem Buch zeigt **gelb** Text in deutscher Sprache.

Printed and bound in China.

The Hanway Press Ltd.

Contenidos

Mapa de las Galápagos
iv
Prólogo
vi
Los creadores de este libro
viii
Agradecimientos
ix
Clave de identificación
xiv
Aves marinas
1
Aves costeras
13
Aves terrestres
21
Mamíferos terrestres
39
Mamíferos marinos
43
Reptiles
51
Plantas de zonas costeras
63
Plantas de zonas áridas
69
Plantas de zonas húmedas
79
Generalidades
88
Bibliografía
121
Índices
122
Los nombres científicos
128

Contents

Map of Galápagos
iv
Foreword
vi
Who created this book
x
Acknowledgements
xi
Keys to the text
xiv
Seabirds
1
Coastal birds
13
Land birds
21
Land mammals
39
Marine mammals
43
Reptiles
51
Coastal plants
63
Arid zone plants
69
Humid zone plants
79
General Information
121
Bibliography
121
Indexes
124
Scientific names
128

Inhalt

Karte von Galápagos
iv
Vorwort
vi
Die Menschen hinter diesem Buch
xii
Danksagungen
xiii
Texterläuterungen
xiv
Meeresvögel
1
Küstenvögel
13
Landvögel
21
Landsäugetiere
39
Meeressäugetiere
43
Reptilien
51
Küstenpflanzen
63
Pflanzen der Trockengebiete
69
Pflanzen der Feuchtgebiete
79
Allgemeine Information
109
Literaturverzeichnis
121
Verzeichnisse
126
Wissenschaftliche bezeichnungen
128

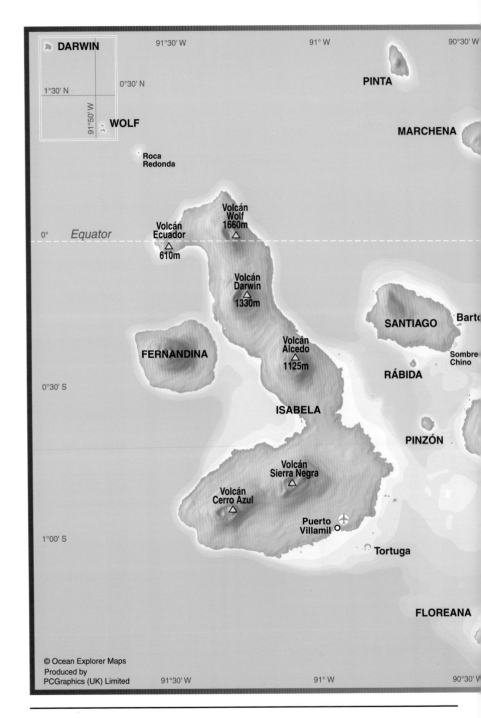

DARWIN

91°30' W   91° W   90°30' W

1°30' N   0°30' N   PINTA

91°50' W   WOLF   MARCHENA

Roca
Redonda

0°   Equator   Volcán   Volcán
                       Ecuador   Wolf
                         △   1660m
                        610m   △

                              Volcán
                              Darwin
                                △
                              1330m
                                              SANTIAGO   Barto

                              Volcán
              FERNANDINA   Alcedo   Sombre
                               △   Chino
                             1125m   RÁBIDA
0°30' S

                         ISABELA
                                              PINZÓN

                          Volcán
                       Sierra Negra
                Volcán   △
              Cerro Azul
                 △
                           Puerto
                           Villamil ○
1°00' S
                              Tortuga

                                              FLOREANA

© Ocean Explorer Maps
Produced by
PCGraphics (UK) Limited   91°30' W   91° W   90°30' W

90° W 89°30' W 89°W

0°30' N

GENOVESA

Galápagos Islands
(Ecuador)

SCALE
Approx 1:1,300,000

Equator 0°

Pacific Ocean

Seymour
BALTRA

0°30' S

Plazas

NTA CRUZ

SAN CRISTÓBAL

uerto
ora

SANTA FÉ

Puerto Baquerizo
Moreno

1°00' S

ESPAÑOLA Gardner

90° W 89°30' W 89°W

Prólogo

La Guía de los animales y plantas de Galápagos, de Nigel Sitwell, viene a completar de manera excepcional las obras ya publicadas sobre este fascinante archipiélago. Escrita de manera accesible y al mismo tiempo única en su género, esta guía trilingüe, que se publica en ingles, español y alemán, facilita la labor de divulgación de las Galápagos a una amplia gama de lectores. Bellamente ilustrada por un equipo de artistas especializados, la guía constituye una herramienta perfecta, tanto para principiantes como para naturalistas experimentados. Las interesantes secciones que hablan de historia, geología, fauna y flora, así como las iniciativas de conservación ambiental, encabezadas por el Parque Nacional de Galápagos y la Fundación Charles Darwin, ofrecen

Foreword

Nigel Sitwell's *Galápagos: Guide to the Animals and Plants* is a welcome and notable addition to the works on this alluring archipelago. Accessibly written yet unique among its genre, this trilingual volume is presented in English, Spanish and German, readily expanding Galápagos knowledge to a broad range of readers. Complemented with lovely illustrations by a team of skilled artists, the book holds appeal for beginners and seasoned naturalists alike.

Cogently written sections on Galápagos history, natural history, wildlife and the conservation initiatives headed by the Galápagos National Park Service and Charles Darwin Foundation provide a concise overview of this storied archipelago. Above all, this guide contributes to our deeper appreciation of

Vorwort

Nigel Sitwells Galápagos: *Tier- und Pflanzenführer* ist eine willkommene und bemerkenswerte Ergänzung zu den Arbeiten über diese verlockende Inselgruppe. Gut verständlich geschrieben und trotzdem einmalig in seiner Art, erscheint dieser Band in englischer, spanischer und deutscher Sprache und macht das Wissen über die Galápagos-Inseln einer Vielfalt von Lesern leicht zugänglich. Das Buch wird ergänzt durch wunderschöne Illustrationen von einer Gruppe begabter Künstler und spricht sowohl Neulinge als auch erfahrene Naturforscher gleichermaßen an.

Überzeugend geschriebene Abschnitte über die Geschichte, die Naturgeschichte, die Tierwelt und die vom Galapagos National Park Service und

una visión general y concisa de este glorioso archipiélago. Ante todo, esta guía ayuda a comprender mejor las razones por las cuales es tan importante conservar y restaurar esas valiosas islas para las futuras generaciones.

Aplaudo con entusiasmo a Nigel y a sus excelentes colaboradores por la labor de creación de este espléndido libro y estoy seguro de que se convertirá en un apreciado compañero de viaje para todos aquellos que visiten o se interesen por la fauna y la flora de las Galápagos.

Dr. J. Gabriel López, PhD
Director Ejecutivo
Fundación Charles Darwin

why these island treasures must be preserved and restored for present and future generations.

I highly commend Nigel and his gifted collaborators for creating this splendid volume and am certain that it will be a welcome companion for all who visit and who care about Galápagos flora and fauna.

J. Gabriel López, PhD
Executive Director
Charles Darwin Foundation

der Charles Darwin Foundation angeführten Naturschutzmaßnahmen geben einen präzisen Überblick über diese sagenumwobene Inselwelt. Vor allem aber trägt dieser Führer zu unserem besseren Verständnis dafür bei, warum diese wertvollen Inseln für jetzige und künftige Generationen erhalten und wiederhergestellt werden müssen.

Ich kann dieses vortreffliche Buch nur wärmstens empfehlen und bin sicher, dass es ein willkommener Begleiter sein wird für alle Besucher, denen die Flora und Fauna der Galápagos-Inseln am Herzen liegt.

Dr. J. Gabriel López
Geschäftsführender Direktor
Charles Darwin Foundation

Los creadores de este libro

Nigel Sitwell El escritor británico, autor y editor de esta obra, es uno de los fundadores del Galápagos Conservation Trust. Tras su primera visita en 1965, ha vuelto a las Galápagos en numerosas ocasiones, la mayoría de las veces como guía turístico. Ha sido galardonado con el premio Order of the Golden Ark, concedido por el Príncipe Bernardo de los Países Bajos, por su labor en la conservación de la naturaleza.

Sarah Darwin La tataranieta de Charles Darwin vive en Londres, donde ejerce una carrera científica y es la autora de las ilustraciones de casi todas las plantas de libro.

Thalia Grant Visitó por primera vez las Galápagos a los seis años de edad, acompañando a sus padres, Peter y Rosemary Grant, al comienzo de su larga carrera de investigación de los pinzones de Darwin. Desde 1996 reside en las Galápagos, donde no ha dejado de dibujar los animales y plantas de las islas. Es autora de las ilustraciones de los pinzones de Darwin que ilustran este libro.

Denys Ovenden Este artista británico lleva unos sesenta años ilustrando la historia natural y sus obras han aparecido en numerosas guías de campo. Denys es el autor de las ilustraciones de los reptiles y mamíferos de este libro.

Maggie Raynor Esta artista británica estudió en el College of Art de Sheffield y en el Royal College of Art de Londres y descubrió su pasión por pintar la naturaleza tras una visita a África. Maggie es la autora de la mayoría de las ilustraciones de las aves de este libro.

Mary Ellen Taylor Nació en Nueva York, donde estudió para artista gráfica y su interés por el turismo de aventura la llevó a instalarse en Ecuador, desde donde visitó las Galápagos como guía naturalista, en numerosas ocasiones. En 2003 se instaló en Londres para estudiar arte botánico en The English Gardening School. Mary Ellen ha ilustrado los helechos y las escalesias de este libro.

Agradecimientos

El autor quisiera agradecer a las siguientes personas por su ayuda en hacer realidad este libro.

Primero debo agradecer a todos los artistas que nos apoyan con sus ilustraciones, ya que estas son la pieza principal de este libro. Al artista Americano y naturalista Roger Tory Peterson cuya *Guía de Campo de Aves* abrió la senda para el desarrollo de las modernas guías de identificación, convencido de que el trabajo artístico, donde es posible, es preferible a las fotografías. De igual manera agradezco a Sarah Darwin, Denys Ovenden, Maggie Raynor, Mary Ellen Taylor y Thalía Grant, algunos de los que han estado esperando mucho tiempo para ver su trabajo en imprenta.

Otros que ofrecieron fotografías y materiales para ser utilizados como referencia para los artistas. Estos incluyen a Tui De Roy, cuya foto permitió a Denys Ovenden pintar a la recientemente descubierta y casi irreal iguana terrestre rosada; Robert C. Dowler quien proporcionó fotos de la poco conocida rata de arroz; Robert A. Thomas, quien asistió con información sobre culebras; y Ole Hamann y Marianne Skaarup Lindhardt quienes ayudaron con las ilustraciones de las Scalesias.

Hay dos personas que han desempeñado un rol clave en la elaboración de este libro. Se trata de Clara Villanueva y Heinke Jäger, quienes tradujeron el texto asociado a las planchas en color al español y al alemán respectivamente. Clara y Heinke también brindaron su colaboración en otros aspectos, por lo que les estoy muy agradecido. Por ejemplo, Heinke Jäger revisó minuciosamente las páginas sobre botánica. Quiero también agradecerles a Anna Belén Carrasco Harcourt y a Alfredo Carrasco por sus traducciones adicionales al español, y a Kerstin Büssenschütt, de Language Marketplace UK Ltd, por sus traducciones adicionales al alemán.

También me gustaría dar las gracias a Linda Cayot, Felipe Cruz y Marco Altamirano Benavides quienes proporcionaron consejos y animo; de la misma forma lo hizo Conley K. McMullen, a quien le agradezco su permiso para usar una serie de los nombres comunes de las plantas que se encuentran en su magnífico libro *Las Plantas en Flor de las Galápagos*, libro que recomiendo a cualquier visitante con interés serio en plantas.

Un gracias enorme a ti Richard Kelly por el diseño de este libro, el mismo que estuvo como proyecto durante varios años; también una dedicación a la memoria de Lars-Eric Lindblad por enviarme a tantos cruceros por las Galápagos durante los años 80 y 90. Finalmente muchas gracias a mi hermano, sin su apoyo en las primeras etapas dudo mucho que este proyecto se hubiera realizado.

Who created this book

Nigel Sitwell is the author of this guidebook. He is a British writer and editor who was one of the founders of the Galapagos Conservation Trust. He first visited Galapagos in 1965, and has made many more visits since then, most of them as the leader of tourist groups. He was awarded the Order of the Golden Ark by Prince Bernhard of the Netherlands for services to wildlife conservation.

Sarah Darwin is a great-great-grandchild of Charles Darwin and lives in London, where she pursues a scientific career. She painted nearly all the plants in this book.

Thalia Grant first went to Galápagos when she was six years old, accompanying her parents, Peter and Rosemary Grant, at the start of their long-term study of Darwin's Finches. She has been sketching Galápagos wildlife for many years and has been a resident there since1996. She painted the Darwin's Finches for this book.

Denys Ovenden is a British artist who has spent about sixty years in natural history illustration, with much of his work appearing in field guides. Denys painted all the reptiles and mammals in this book.

Maggie Raynor is a British artist who studied at the Sheffield College of Art, and later at the Royal College of Art in London. She was inspired to paint wildlife following a visit to Africa. Maggie painted most of the birds for this book.

Mary Ellen Taylor was born in New York, where she trained as a graphic artist. An interest in adventure tourism led her to settle in Ecuador, where she visited Galápagos many times as a naturalist guide. In 2003 she moved to London to pursue Botanical Painting at the English Gardening School. Mary Ellen painted the Ferns and Scalesias for this book.

Acknowledgements

The editor would like to thank the following people for their help in making this book a reality.

First of all I must thank the artists whose illustrations are the centrepiece of this book. The American artist and naturalist Roger Tory Peterson, whose *Field Guide to the Birds* led the way in modern identification guides, believed that artwork is preferable to photographs where possible. So I say a warm thank you to Sarah Darwin, Denys Ovenden, Maggie Raynor, Mary Ellen Taylor, and Thalia Grant, some of whom have been waiting a very long time to see their work in print.

Others offered photographs and other material to be used as artists' references. These include Tui De Roy, whose photo enabled Denys Ovenden to portray the newly discovered and almost surreally pink land iguana; Robert C. Dowler, who provided pictures of the very little known rice rats; Robert A Thomas, who assisted with information about the snakes; and Ole Hamann and Marianne Skaarup Lindhardt who helped us illustrate the Scalesias.

There are two people who have played a key role in the production of this book. They are Clara Villanueva and Heinke Jäger who translated the text associated with the colour plates from English into Spanish and German respectively. Clara and Heinke assisted in other ways for which I am very grateful.For example the botanical pages have been carefully checked by Heinke Jäger.Thanks also to Anna Belén Carrasco Harcourt and Alfredo Carrasco for additional translations into Spanish while additional translations into German were provided by Kerstin Büssenschütt of Language Marketplace UK Ltd.

I would also like to thank Linda Cayot, Felipe Cruz, and Marco Altamirano Benavides who provided advice and encouragement, as did Conley K. McMullen, to whom I am grateful for permission to use a number of the common names for plant species in his splendid book *Flowering Plants of the Galápagos*, which I recommend to any visitor with a serious interest in plants.

Next, a very big thank you to Richard Kelly who designed the book, and stayed with the task through its ups and downs over the years; and a dedication to the memory of Lars-Eric Lindblad for sending me on so many Galápagos cruises in the 1980s and 1990s. And finally very many thanks to my brother Denis for his great support in the early stages, without which I doubt that this project would ever have been undertaken.

Die Menschen hinter diesem Buch

Nigel Sitwell ist der Autor und Redakteur. Er ist ein britischer Schriftsteller und war einer der Gründer des Galápagos Conservation Trust. Er besuchte Galápagos zum ersten Mal im Jahre 1965 und ist seitdem viele Male zurückgekehrt, meistens als Führer von Reisegruppen. Er erhielt von Prinz Bernhard der Niederlande den „Orden der Goldenen Arche" zur Anerkennung seiner Verdienste um den Artenschutz.

Sarah Darwin ist die Ururenkelin von Charles Darwin und lebt in London, wo sie eine wissenschaftliche Laufbahn verfolgt. Fast alle Pflanzenabbildungen in diesem Buch wurden von ihr gemalt.

Thalia Grant reiste zum ersten Mal im Alter von sechs Jahren mit ihren Eltern Peter und Rosemary Grant nach Galápagos, als diese ihre Langzeitstudie der Darwins Finken begannen. Sie zeichnet seit vielen Jahren die Tierwelt der Galápagos-Inseln und lebt dort seit 1996. Von ihr stammen die Abbildungen der Darwins Finken für dieses Buch.

Denys Ovenden ist ein britischer Künstler, der auf gut sechzig Jahre naturgeschichtlicher Illustrationen zurückblicken kann; viele seiner Arbeiten finden sich in Naturführern. Er malte alle Abbildungen der Reptilien und Säugetiere für dieses Buch.

Maggie Raynor ist eine britische Künstlerin, die zunächst am Sheffield College of Art und später am Royal College of Art in London studierte. Eine Reise nach Afrika inspirierte sie zum Malen wilder Tiere. Von ihr stammen die Abbildungen der meisten Vögel in diesem Buch.

Mary Ellen Taylor wurde in New York geboren, wo sie eine Ausbildung zur Grafikerin machte. Durch ihr Interesse an Abenteuerreisen ließ sie sich in Ecuador nieder, wo sie Galápagos viele Male als Naturführerin besuchte. 2003 zog sie nach London, um an der English Gardening School botanische Malerei zu studieren. Die Abbildungen der Farne und Scalesien in diesem Buch wurden von ihr gemalt.

Danksagungen

Der Redakteur möchte den folgenden Personen für Ihre Hilfe bei der Verwirklichung dieses Buches danken.

Zuallererst muss ich den Künstlern danken, deren Illustrationen der Mittelpunkt dieses Buches sind. Der amerikanische Künstler und Naturforscher Roger Tory Peterson, dessen „Einführung in die Vogelkunde" richtungsweisend für moderne Bestimmungsbücher war, vertrat die Ansicht, dass Zeichnungen wann immer möglich Fotografien vorzuziehen sind. Ich bedanke mich somit ganz herzlich bei Sarah Darwin, Denys Ovenden, Maggie Raynor, Mary Ellen Taylor und Thalia Grant, von denen einige sehr lange auf den Abdruck Ihrer Arbeiten gewartet haben.

Andere haben Fotografien und sonstige Materialien als Grundlagen für die Arbeiten der Künstler zur Verfügung gestellt. Darunter auch Tui De Roy, mit dessen Foto Denys Ovenden den kürzlich entdeckten und fast schon übernatürlich rosafarbenen Landleguan porträtieren konnte; Robert C. Dowler, der Bilder von den nur wenig bekannten Reisratten zur Verfügung stellte; Robert A. Thomas, der uns mit Informationen über die Schlangen unterstützte; und Ole Hamann und Marianne Skaarup Lindhardt, die uns bei den Illustrationen der Scalesien halfen.

Zwei Personen haben bei der Entstehung dieses Buches eine Schlüsselrolle gespielt: Clara Villanueva und Heinke Jäger, die die Texte für die Farbtafeln vom Englischen ins Spanische bzw. Deutsche übersetzt haben. Clara und Heinke haben uns auch auf andere Weise unterstützt, wofür ich ihnen sehr dankbar bin. So wurden zum Beispiel die Botanikseiten sorgfältig von Heinke Jäger überprüft. Vielen Dank auch an Anna Belén Carrasco Harcourt und Alfredo Carrasco für zusätzliche Übersetzungen ins Spanische, während zusätzliche Übersetzungen ins Deutsche von Kerstin Büssenschütt (Language Marketplace UK Ltd.) stammen.

Außerdem möchte ich Linda Cayot, Felipe Cruz und Marco Altamirano Benavides für ihren Rat und ihre Unterstützung danken, ebenso wie Conley K. McMullen, dem ich dankbar bin für die Erlaubnis zur Verwendung einer Reihe von Trivialnamen für Pflanzenarten aus seinem großartigen Buch „Flowering Plants of the Galápagos", das ich jedem Besucher mit ernsthaftem Interesse an Pflanzen ans Herz legen möchte.

Dann noch ein großes Dankeschön an Richard Kelly, der dieses Buch gestaltet hat und durch das Auf und Ab der Jahre mit dabeigeblieben ist; und eine Widmung zum Gedenken an Lars-Eric Lindblad, der mich in den achtziger und neunziger Jahren auf so viele Galápagos-Reisen geschickt hat. Und schließlich vielen Dank an meinen Bruder Denis, ohne dessen großartige Unterstützung in der Anfangsphase dieses Projekt wahrscheinlich niemals zustande gekommen wäre.

Clave de identificación

Para ahorrar espacio hemos utilizado como clave de identificación letras y números que describen la categoría y la situación de cada especie animal y vegetal en las islas Galápagos.

Las letras indican la categoría general de las especies animales y vegetales de las islas Galápagos.

E Especies endémicas

Se Subespecies endémicas

N Nativas

R Residentes

M Migratorias

V Vagabundas

I Introducidas

Los números indican su situación en las islas Galápagos, siguiendo los parámetros oficiales de la UICN (Unión Internacional para la Conservación de la Naturaleza) en las primeras cuatro categorías:

1 En grave peligro de extinción

2 En peligro de extinción

3 Vulnerables

4 Casi amenazadas

5 Raras

6 Poco comunes

7 Bastante comunes

8 Comunes

9 Abundantes

❖ Este símbolo indica las zonas o el hábitat donde puede verse cada especie.

Key to the text

To save space, we have used the following letters and numerals to indicate the status of these animal and plant species in Galápagos.

Letters indicate their general status in the archipelago's wildlife populations.

E Endemic species

Es Endemic subspecies

N Native

R Resident

M Migrant

V Vagrant

I Introduced

Numerals indicate their numerical abundance in Galápagos, using designations of the International Union for Conservation of Nature (IUCN) in the first four categories.

1 Critically endangered

2 Endangered

3 Vulnerable

4 Near threatened

5 Rare

6 Uncommon

7 Fairly common

8 Common

9 Abundant

❖ This symbol indicates the areas or habitats where the species are most likely to be seen.

Texterläuterungen

Um Platz zu sparen, haben wir die folgenden Buchstaben und Zahlen gewählt, um den Status der Tiere und Pflanzen auf Galápagos anzuzeigen.

Buchstaben zeigen ihren allgemeinen Status in der Fauna im Archipel an.

E Endemische Arten

Es Endemische Unterarten

N Einheimisch

R Standvogel

M Zugvogel

V Irrgast

I Eingeführte Art

Zahlen zeigen ihre Häufigkeit in Galápagos an, unter Verwendung der offiziellen Bezeichnung en der ersten vier Kategorien (unten) durch die Weltnaturschutzunion (IUCN)

1 Kritisch gefährdet

2 Gefährdet

3 Verletzbar

4 Potentiell bedroht

5 Rar

6 Selten

7 Ziemlich häufig

8 Häufig

9 Sehr häufig

❖ Dieses Symbol zeigt an, in welchen Gebieten oder Habitaten die Wahrscheinlichkeit am größten ist, die Arten zu sehen.

AVES MARINAS

SEABIRDS

MEERESVÖGEL

1 Pingüino de Galápagos

E-2 La única especie de pingüino que habita al norte del Ecuador y una de las más pequeñas.

❖ Costas de Fernandina, Isabela, Bartolomé y Sombrero Chino.

2 Albatros de Galápagos

N-1 La especie de albatros más septentrional que existe. Casi toda la población mundial anida en las Galápagos.

❖ Costas de Española, aunque normalmente no se ven de enero a marzo.

3 Pufino de Galápagos

E-8 Esta pequeña ave marina se alimenta en grandes bandadas.

❖ Muy extendida a lo largo de las costas marinas.

1 Galápagos Penguin

E-2 The only penguin species found north of the Equator, and one of the smallest.

❖ Coasts of Fernandina, Isabela, Bartolomé, & Sombrero Chino.

2 Waved Albatross

N-1 Most northerly albatross species. Almost the whole world population breeds in Galápagos.

❖ Coast of Española, but seldom seen January-March.

3 Galápagos Shearwater

E-8 A small shearwater that feeds in large flocks.

❖ Widespread along sea coasts.

1 Galápagospinguin

E-2 Der einzige Pinguin, der nördlich des Äquators vorkommt, und auch einer der kleinsten.

❖ Küsten von Fernandina, Isabela, Bartolomé und Sombrero Chino.

2 Galápagosalbatros

N-3 Die am nördlichsten vorkommende Albatrosart. Fast die gesamte weltweite Population brütet auf Galápagos.

❖ Küste von Española, aber kaum anzutreffen von Januar-März.

3 Galápagos-sturmtaucher

E-8 Dieser kleine Seevogel fischt in großen Schwärmen.

❖ Weit verbreitet an Meeresküsten.

1 *Spheniscus mendiculus*

2 *Phoebastria irrorata*

3 *Puffinus subalaris*

1 Petrel Patapegada

E-1 En las Galápagos sólo existen cuatro colonias de esta ave marina nocturna.

❖ Tierras altas de San Cristóbal, Santa Cruz, Santiago y Floreana.

2 Petrel de Elliot

Se-8 Aunque hay miles de estas aves en las Galápagos nunca se ha encontrado ningún nido.

❖ Muy extendidas cerca de las orillas.

3 Petrel de Madeira

R-8 El más grande de los petreles de Galápagos. Dos poblaciones utilizan los mismos nidos pero en diferentes épocas del año.

❖ Muy extendidas en las costas marinas.

4 Petrel de Galápagos

Se-4 Esta especie se alimenta por la noche y puede verse alrededor de los nidos durante el día.

❖ Costas de Genovesa e Isla Pitt (San Cristóbal).

5 Petrel de Leach

V-5 Un visitante ocasional, muy semejante al Petrel de Madeira.

❖ Costas marinas.

6 Pufino Negro

N-6 Ave marina de vuelo rápido que suele verse en pequeños grupos.

❖ Costas marinas.

1 Galápagos Petrel

E-1 There are only four colonies of this shy, nocturnal seabird in Galápagos.

❖ Highlands of San Cristóbal, Santa Cruz, Santiago, Floreana.

2 Elliot's (White-vented) Storm Petrel

Es-8 There are thousands of these small petrels in Galápagos, but no nest has ever been found.

❖ Widespread close to shore.

3 Madeiran (Band-rumped) Storm Petrel

R-8 Largest Galápagos storm petrel. Two populations use the same nesting sites, but at different times of the year.

❖ Widespread on sea coasts.

4 Galápagos (Wedge-rumped) Storm Petrel

Es-4 This species feeds at night and is seen around the nest sites during the day.

❖ Sea coasts at Genovesa and Isla Pitt (San Cristóbal).

5 Leach's Storm Petrel

V-5 An occasional visitor; very similar to the Madeiran storm petrel.

❖ Sea coasts.

6 Sooty Shearwater

N-6 Fast-flying shearwater that is regularly seen in small numbers.

❖ Sea coasts.

1 Galápagos-Sturmvogel

E-1 Es gibt nur vier Kolonien dieses scheuen, nachtaktiven Seevogels auf Galápagos.

❖ Hochland von San Cristóbal, Santa Cruz, Santiago, Floreana.

2 Elliot-Sturmschwalbe

Es-8 Es gibt Tausende dieser kleinen Sturmvögel im Galápagos-Archipel, aber es wurde noch nie ein Nest gefunden.

❖ Weit verbreitet in Küstennähe.

3 Madeira-Wellenläufer

R-8 Größter Sturmvogel auf Galápagos. Zwei Populationen benutzen dasselbe Brutgebiet, aber zu unterschiedlichen Zeiten im Jahr.

❖ Weit verbreitet an Meeresküsten.

4 Galápagos-Wellenläufer

Es-8 Dieser Vogel ernährt sich nachts und kann bei Tage in der Nähe der Bruthöhlen beobachtet werden.

❖ Meeresküste von Genovesa, Isla Pitt (San Cristóbal).

5 Leach-Wallenläufer

V-5 Ein durchziehender Gastvogel, dem Madeira-Wellenläufer sehr ähnlich.

❖ Meeresküsten.

6 Dunkler Sturmtaucher

N-6 Schnell fliegender Sturmtaucher, der regelmäßig in geringer Anzahl beobachten werden kann.

❖ Meeresküsten.

1 *Pterodroma phaeopygia*

2 *Oceanites gracilis galapagoensis*

4 *Oceanodroma tethys tethys*

3 *Oceanodroma castro*

5 *Oceanodroma leucorhoa*

6 *Puffinus griseus*

1 Piquero de Patas Azules

Se-8 La mayor parte de la población mundial de esta ave se encuentra en las Galápagos. Se alimentan cerca de la orilla.

❖ Muy extendida en las costas marinas al sur del Ecuador.

2 Piquero de Nazca

R-8 Esta especie se alimenta en el archipiélago pero raramente cerca de la orilla.

❖ Costas marinas, especialmente en Española, San Cristóbal y Genovesa.

3 Piquero de Patas Rojas

Se-7 Esta especie anida en árboles y arbustos y se alimenta lejos de la tierra firme. Existen dos variedades: marrón (3a) y blanca (3b). En las Galápagos el 95% de estas aves son marrones pero en otros lugares el 95% son blancas.

❖ Costas marinas, especialmente en Genovesa, San Cristóbal, Seymour Norte, Darwin y Wolf.

4 Pájaro Tropical o Piloto

R-7 Esta elegante ave marina blanca anida en las grietas de las rocas.

❖ Costas marinas, especialmente en Genovesa y Plazas.

1 Blue-footed Booby

Es-8 Most of the world population of this bird is found in Galápagos. They feed close to shore.

❖ Widespread on sea coasts south of the Equator.

2 Nazca Booby

R-8 This species feeds within the archipelago, but seldom close to shore.

❖ Sea coasts, especially Española, San Cristóbal, Genovesa.

3 Red-footed Booby

Es-7 This species nests in trees and bushes and feeds well away from land. There are two varieties: brown (3a) and white (3b). In Galapagos 95% of birds are brown, but elsewhere 95% are white.

❖ Sea coasts, especially Genovesa, San Cristóbal, North Seymour, Darwin, Wolf.

4 Red-billed Tropicbird

R-7 This elegant white seabird nests in crevices in rocks.

❖ Sea coasts, especially Genovesa, Plazas.

1 Blaufußtölpel

Es-8 Der größte Teil der weltweiten Population dieses Vogels ist auf Galápagos beheimatet. Sie fischen in Küstennähe.

❖ Weit verbreitet an Meeresküsten südlich des Äquators.

2 Nazcatölpel

R-8 Diese Art fischt innerhalb des Archipels, aber selten in Küstennähe.

❖ Meeresküsten, besonders Española, San Cristóbal, Genovesa.

3 Rotfußtölpel

Es-7 Diese Art brütet auf Bäumen und Sträuchern und fischt fernab der Küsten. Es gibt zwei Formen: braun (3a) und weiß (3b). Auf Galápagos sind 95 % der Vögel braun, aber anderswo sind 95 % weiß.

❖ Meeresküsten, besonders Genovesa, San Cristóbal, North Seymour, Darwin, Wolf.

4 Rotschnabel-Tropikvogel

R-7 Dieser elegante, weiße Seevogel brütet in Felsspalten.

❖ Meeresküsten, besonders Genovesa, Plazas

1 *Sula nebouxii excisa*

2 *Sula granti*

3a

3b

3 *Sula sula websteri*

4 *Phaethon aethereus*

1 Pelícano Café

Se-8 Esta ave tiene una envergadura de dos metros y se alimenta zambulléndose en el agua. El de la ilustración exhibe el plumaje de cría.

❖ Costas marinas.

2 Cormorán no Volador

E-2 Esta ave dejó de volar debido a la ausencia de predadores y a la abundancia de comida. Tras el baño se seca las alas como los otros cormoranes.

❖ Costas marinas de Fernandina e Isabela.

3 Fragata Común

Se-7 Esta ave no puede ni caminar ni nadar pero posee una gran potencia de vuelo que le permite alimentarse atrapando su presa en la superficie del mar y robándosela a otras aves marinas. El macho (3a) hincha la bolsa roja de la garganta para exhibirse y atraer a las hembras (3b). (3c) Inmaturo.

❖ Muy extendida en las costas marinas.

4 Fragata Real

Se-7 Esta especie depende más de robarle el alimento a otras aves que la Fragata Común. Las plumas dorsales del macho (4a) son más bien violáceas, comparadas con las plumas verdes de las otras especies. Hembra (4b). Inmaturo (4c).

❖ Muy extendida en las costas marinas.

1 Brown Pelican

Es-8 This bird has a wingspan of two metres and feeds by plunge diving. The bird shown here is in breeding plumage.

❖ Sea coasts.

2 Flightless Cormorant

E-2 The absence of predators and plentiful food probably led to this bird becoming flightless. It dries its wings after returning to shore, like other cormorants.

❖ Sea coasts of Fernandina and Isabela.

3 Great Frigatebird

R-7 This bird cannot walk or swim, but is a powerful flier, picking food from the surface of the sea, and also stealing it from other seabirds. The male (3a) inflates his red throat pouch in the breeding season to attract females (3b). The bird (3c) is a juvenile.

❖ Widespread on sea coasts.

4 Magnificent Frigatebird

Es-7 This species depends more on stealing from other birds than the previous species. The male (4a) has purplish feathers on its back compared to the greenish feathers of the other species. Female (4b), Juvenile (4c).

❖ Widespread on sea coasts.

1 Galápagosbraunpelikan

Es-8 Dieser Vogel hat eine Flügelspannweite von 2 m und fischt durch Sturztauchen. Der hier gezeigte Vogel befindet sich im Brutgefieder.

❖ Meeresküsten.

2 Galápagoskormoran

E-2 Die Abwesenheit von Prädatoren und ein reichhaltiges Nahrungsangebot haben wahrscheinlich zur Entwicklung der Flugunfähigkeit dieses Vogels geführt. Sie trocknen ihre Flügel nach Rückkehr zur Küste, wie auch andere Kormorane (Scharben).

❖ Meeresküste von Fernandina und Isabela.

3 Bindenfregattvogel

Es-7 Dieser Vogel kann weder laufen noch schwimmen, ist aber ein kräftiger Flieger, der seine Nahrung von der Meeresoberfläche aufpickt oder diese auch anderen Seevögeln abjagt. Während der Brutzeit bläht das Männchen (3a) seinen roten Kehlsack auf, um Weibchen anzulocken (3b). Hier ein Jungvogel (3c).

❖ Weit verbreitet an Meeresküsten.

4 Prachtfregattvogel

Es-7 Diese Art ist noch mehr vom Abjagen der Nahrung anderer Vögel abhängig als die vorherige Art. Das Gefieder auf dem Rücken des Männchens (4a) ist purpurfarben, bei der anderen Art ist es grünlich. Weibchen (4b), Jungvogel (4c).

❖ Weit verbreitet an Meeresküsten.

1 *Pelecanus occidentalis urinator*

2 *Phalacrocorax harrisi*

3 *Fregata minor*

3a

3b

3c

4b

4a

4c

4b

3b

4 *Fregata m. magnificens*

1 Gaviota de Cola Bifurcada

R-8 La única gaviota nocturna del mundo y prácticamente endémica en las Galápagos. Adulto (1a) e inmaturo (1b).

❖ Muy extendida a lo largo de las costas marinas.

2 Gaviota de Franklin

M-7 Suele permanecer en las Galápagos de octubre a marzo.

❖ Costas marinas durante el invierno septentrional.

3 Nodi o Gaviotín Pardo

Se-7 Ave de color muy oscuro que acompaña a menudo a los pelícanos pescadores.

❖ Cría en pequeñas cuevas en los acantilados marinos.

4 Gaviota de Lava

E-3 Esta especie cuenta con una población total de 400 parejas pero parece estable. Adulto (4a) e inmaturo (4b).

❖ Muy extendida en las playas.

5 Gaviotín Tiznado

R-6 Gaviotín con distintivo plumaje blanco y negro.

❖ Existe en gran número en Darwin pero apenas se ve en ningún otro lugar.

6 Gaviotín Rea

M-6 Gaviotín de gran tamaño que llega de enero a marzo.

❖ Costas marinas.

1 Swallow-tailed Gull

R-8 The world's only nocturnal gull, and almost only found in Galápagos. Adult (1a) and juvenile (1b).

❖ Widespread along sea coasts.

2 Franklin's Gull

M-7 A regular visitor to Galápagos October-March.

❖ Along sea coasts in the northern winter.

3 Brown Noddy

Es-7 A very dark-coloured bird that often accompanies fishing pelicans.

❖ Breeds in small caves in sea cliffs.

4 Lava Gull

E-3 This species has a total population of about 400 pairs, but seems stable. Adult (4a) and juvenile (4b).

❖ Widespread on Galápagos beaches.

5 Sooty Tern

R-6 A tern with distinctive black and white plumage.

❖ Breeds in large numbers on Darwin, but seldom seen elsewhere.

6 Royal tern

M-6 A large tern that visits in January-March.

❖ Sea coasts.

1 Gabelschwanzmöwe

R-8 Weltweit einzige nachtaktive Möwe und kommt fast nur auf Galápagos vor. Altvogel (1a) und Jungvogel (1b).

❖ Weit verbreitet an Meeresküsten.

2 Franklin-Möwe

M-7 Regelmäßiger Besucher der Galápagos-Inseln von Oktober bis März.

❖ Entlang von Meeresküsten während des Winters der nördlichen Hemisphäre.

3 Noddi-Seeschwalbe

Es-7 Sehr dunkel gefärbter Vogel, der oftmals fischende Pelikane begleitet.

❖ Brütet in kleinen Höhlen am Meereskliff.

4 Lavamöwe

E-3 Diese Art bsteht nur aus einer Gesamtpopulation von ungefähr 400 Brutpaaren, Population scheint aber stabil zu sein. Altvogel (4a) und Jungvogel (4b).

❖ Weit verbreitet an Galápagos-Stränden.

5 Rußseeschwalbe

R-6 Seeschwalbe mit charakteristischem schwarz-weißem Gefieder.

❖ Brütet in großer Zahl auf Darwin, wird nur selten woanders gesehen.

6 Königsseeschwalbe

M-6 Große Seeschwalbe, die von Januar bis März anzutreffen ist.

❖ Meeresküsten.

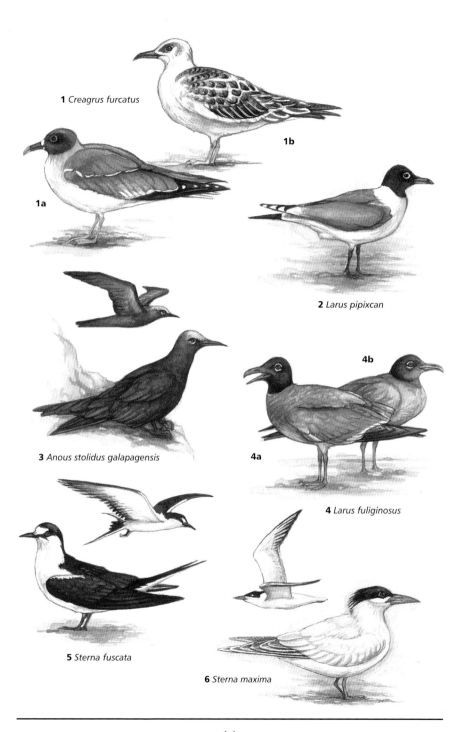

1 *Creagrus furcatus*

1b

1a

2 *Larus pipixcan*

3 *Anous stolidus galapagensis*

4b

4a

4 *Larus fuliginosus*

5 *Sterna fuscata*

6 *Sterna maxima*

AVES COSTERAS

COASTAL BIRDS

KÜSTENVÖGEL

1 Garza Morena

Se-6 La garza más grande de Las Galápagos llega a medir casi un metro de altura.

❖ Muy extendida en lagunas costeras y manglares.

2 Garcita Blanca

V-5 Esta visitante es semejante a la Garza Vaquera pero tiene las patas y el pico negros.

❖ Zonas costeras.

3 Garza Vaquera

R-7 Estas aves llegaron por primera vez a Las Galápagos en 1964. Se ven sobre todo en zonas agrícolas. Plumaje habitual (3a) y plumaje en época de cría (3b).

❖ Tierras altas y cerca de las lagunas costeras.

4 Garza Blanca.

R-6 Esta garza totalmente blanca, es casi tan alta como la Garza Morena.

❖ Lagunas costeras, manglares y zonas agrícolas.

5 Huaque o Garza Nocturna

Se-7 Esta garza se alimenta principalmente de noche. Ejemplar adulto (5a) e inmaturo (5b).

❖ Zonas costeras.

6 Garza de Lava

E-7 Esta garza es semejante a la Garcita Estriada y se ve a menudo acechando a su presa en las lagunas costeras.

❖ Muy extendida en zonas costeras.

7 Garcita Estriada

R-6 Los inmaturos se parecen mucho a la Garza de Lava pero los adultos tienen el plumaje a rayas.

❖ Zonas costeras.

1 Great Blue Heron

Es-6 This is the largest heron in Galápagos, standing nearly one metre tall.

❖ Widespread in coastal lagoons and mangroves.

2 Snowy Egret

V-5 This visitor is similar to the cattle egret, but has a black bill and legs.

❖ Coastal areas.

3 Cattle Egret

R-7 These birds first appeared in Galápagos in 1964. They are mostly seen in the agricultural areas. Non-breeding plumage (3a) and breeding plumage (3b).

❖ Highlands, and also near coastal lagoons.

4 Great Egret

R-6 This all-white heron is nearly as tall as the great blue heron.

❖ Coastal lagoons, mangroves, and agricultural areas.

5 Yellow-crowned Night Heron

Es-7 This heron feeds mainly at night. Adult (5a) and juvenile (5b).

❖ Coastal areas.

6 Lava Heron

E-7 This small heron is often seen stalking prey in coastal lagoons.

❖ Widespread in coastal areas.

7 Striated Heron

R-6 Juveniles are very similar to the lava heron, but the adults have heavy streaking.

❖ Coastal areas.

1 Amerikanischer Graureiher

Es-6 Aufrecht stehend etwa 1 m groß, dieses ist der größte Reiher auf Galápagos.

❖ Weit verbreitet an Küstenlagunen und in Mangrovengebieten.

2 Schmuckreiher

V-5 Dieser durchziehende Gast ähnelt dem Kuhreiher, hat aber einen schwarzen Schnabel und schwarze Beine.

❖ Küstenregionen.

3 Kuhreiher

R-7 Diese Vögel erreichten Galápagos im Jahre 1964. Sie sind vor allem in der landwirtschaftlichen Zone zu beobachten. Federkleid außerhalb (3a) und während der Brutzeit (3b).

❖ Hochland und auch in der Nähe von Küstenlagunen.

4 Silberreiher

R-6 Dieser weiße Reiher ist fast so groß wie der Amerikanische Graureiher.

❖ Küstenlagunen, Mangroven- und landwirtschaftliche Gebiete.

5 Nachtreiher

Es-7 Dieser Reiher fischt hauptsächlich nachts. Hier gezeigt als adulter (5a) und als juveniler Vogel (5b).

❖ Küstenregionen.

6 Lavareiher

E-7 Dieser kleine Reiher ähnelt dem Mangrovenreiher und kann oft beobachtet werden, wie er seine Beute in Küstenlagunen belauert.

❖ Weit verbreitet in Küstenregionen.

7 Mangrovenreiher

R-6 Juvenile Vögel sehen dem Lava-oder Galápagosreiher sehr ähnlich, aber die adulten Vögel sind kräftig gestreift.

❖ Küstenregionen.

1 *Ardea herodias cognata*

2 *Egretta thula*

3 *Bubulcus ibis*

3a

3b

5a

7 *Butorides striata*

5b

4 *Casmerodius albus*

5 *Nyctanassa violaceus pauper*

6 *Butorides sundevalli*

15

1 Flamenco Mayor

Se-6 Pueden verse en pequeños grupos en las lagunas salobres, donde se alimentan de diminutos crustáceos.

❖ Lagunas costeras.

2 Patillo

Se-7 Este pato de tamaño mediano se alimenta en la superficie del agua pero también se sumerge en los lagos en busca de alimento.

❖ Zonas costeras y tierras altas; Santa Cruz, Isabela, Santiago, San Cristóbal.

3 Cerceta Aliazul

V-6 Pato de pequeño tamaño que muestra un distintivo color azul en las alas delanteras cuando vuela.

❖ Lagunas costeras pero también en estanques en las tierras altas.

4 Ostrero

Se-6 Gran zancuda con un pico largo y rojo. Se ven normalmente en parejas.

❖ Muy extendida en las costas marinas.

1 American Flamingo

Es-6 Small groups are seen in brackish lagoons, where they feed on micro-crustaceans.

❖ Coastal lagoons.

2 White-cheeked (Galápagos) Pintail

Es-7 A medium-sized duck that feeds at the surface, but also dives for food in lagoons.

❖ Coastal areas and highlands; Santa Cruz, Isabela, Santiago, San Cristóbal.

3 Blue-winged Teal

V-6 Small duck with distinctive blue fore-wing in flight, but seldom seen.

❖ Coastal lagoons, but also ponds in the highlands.

4 American Oystercatcher

Es-6 Large wader with a long red bill. Usually seen in pairs.

❖ Sea coasts; widespread.

1 Galápagosflamingo

Es-6 Kleine Gruppen können in brackigen Lagunen beobachtet werden, wo sie sich von kleinen Krustentieren ernähren.

❖ Küstenlagunen.

2 Galápagos-Bahamaente

Es-7 Eine mittelgroße Ente, die sich an der Wasseroberfläche ernährt, aber auch nach Futter in Lagunen taucht.

❖ Küstenregionen und Hochland; Santa Cruz, Isabela, Santiago, San Cristóbal.

3 Blauflügelente

V-6 Kleine Ente, blauer Vorderflügel deutlich während des Fluges zu sehen.

❖ Küstenlagunen, aber auch Teiche im Hochland.

4 Braunmantel-Austernfischer

Es-6 Großer Watvogel mit einem langen, roten Schnabel. Meist in Paaren zu beobachten.

❖ Küstenregionen, weit verbreitet.

1 *Phoenicopterus ruber glyphorhynchus*

3 *Anas discors*

2 *Anas bahamensis galapapagensis*

4 *Haematopus palliatus*

1 Falaropo Norteño

M-8 Pequeña zancuda que gira en el agua mientras se alimenta. Este es el plumaje habitual que exhibe cuando no es temporada de cría.

❖ Muy extendida en las zonas costeras.

2 Chorlitejo

M-7 Gran zancuda que muestra unas inconfundibles manchas alares cuando vuela. Este es el plumaje habitual que exhibe cuando no es temporada de cría.

❖ Zonas costeras.

3 Tero real

R-6 Gran zancuda delgada, de patas largas rosadas y pico largo y puntiagudo.

❖ Muy extendida en las zonas costeras.

4 Errante

M-8 Esta zancuda de tamaño mediano es una visitante habitual en Las Galápagos. Plumaje de la temporada de cría (4a) y plumaje habitual (4b).

❖ Costas rocosas.

5 Zarapito

M-7 Gran zancuda con pico curvado hacia abajo. Su señal de llamada consiste en silbidos rápidos.

❖ Costas rocosas y alrededor de los estanques de las tierras altas.

6 Falaropo de Wilson

M-7 Ave de gran tamaño con patas largas y pico recto y delgado. Este es el plumaje que exhibe habitualmente cuando no es temporada de cría.

❖ Principalmente en las lagunas costeras.

1 Red-necked Phalarope

M-8 Small wader that spins in the water while feeding. This is its non-breeding plumage.

❖ Coastal areas; widespread.

2 Willett

M-7 Large wader with unmistakable wing pattern in flight. This is its non-breeding plumage.

❖ Coastal areas.

3 Black-necked Stilt

R-6 Large slim wader with long pink legs and long and pointed bill.

❖ Coastal areas; widespread.

4 Wandering Tattler

M-8 Medium-sized wader, and a common visitor to Galápagos. Shown here in breeding (4a) and non-breeding plumage (4b).

❖ Rocky coasts.

5 Whimbrel

M-7 Large wader with down-curved bill, and a call of rapid whistles.

❖ Rocky coasts, and around ponds in the highlands.

6 Wilson's Phalarope

M-7 Large bird with long legs and straight, thin bill. This is its non-breeding plumage.

❖ Mainly coastal lagoons.

1 Odinshühnchen

M-8 Kleiner Watvogel, der während des Fischens auf dem Wasser kreist. Hier gezeigt im Federkleid außerhalb der Brutzeit.

❖ Küstenregionen, weit erbreitet.

2 Schlammtreter

M-7 Großer Watvogel mit unverwechselbarer Flügelzeichnung während des Fluges. Hier gezeigt im Federkleid außerhalb der Brutzeit.

❖ Küstenregionen.

3 Schwarznacken-Stelzenläufer

R-6 Großer, schlanker Watvogel mit langen pinkfarbenen Beinen und spitz zulaufendem Schnabel.

❖ Küstenregionen, weit erbreitet.

4 Wanderwasserläufer

M-8 Mittelgroßer Watvogel und ein häufiger Gast auf Galápagos. Hier gezeigt im Brutgefieder (4a) und außerhalb der Brutzeit (4b).

❖ Steinige Küsten.

5 Regenbrachvogel

M-7 Großer Watvogel mit abwärts gebogenem Schnabel und mit einem Ruf bestehend aus schnellen Pfeiftönen.

❖ Steinige Küsten und Teiche im Hochland.

6 Wilsonwassertreter

M-7 Großer Vogel mit langen Beinen und einem geraden, schmalen Schnabel. Hier gezeigt im Federkleid außerhalb der Brutzeit.

❖ Meist an Küstenlagunen.

1 *Phalaropus lobatus*

2 *Catoptrophorus semipalmatus*

3 *Himantopus mexicanus*

4a

4b

4 *Heteroscelus incanus*

5 *Numenius phaeopus*

6 *Phalaropus tricolor*

AVES TERRESTRES

LAND BIRDS

LANDVÖGEL

1 Correlino

M-7 Pequeña y activa ave zancuda con plumaje en temporada de cría (1a) y el resto del año (1b).

❖ En las costas marinas.

2 Chorlitejo Semipalmado

M-7 Zancuda robusta con un característico collar. Plumaje en época de cría (2a) y el resto del año (2b).

❖ En las costas marinas y en las charcas de las tierras altas.

3 Playero Enano

M-6 Diminuta zancuda de patas amarillentas.

❖ En las costas marinas y en las lagunas.

4 Playero Cabezón

M-6 Zancuda de tamaño mediano con plumaje en temporada de cría (4a) y el resto del año (4b).

❖ En las costas marinas y lagunas.

5 Chorlito de Rompientes

M-5 Ave zancuda pequeña y oscura con plumaje en temporada de cría (5a) y el resto del año (5b).

❖ Orillas rocosas.

6 Playero Común

M-8 Zancuda pequeña y activa que corretea por la orilla persiguiendo las olas. Plumaje en temporada de cría (6a) y el resto del año (6b).

❖ En las costas marinas.

7 Vuelvepiedras

M-8 Zancuda de patas anaranjadas y plumaje característico en temporada de cría (7a). El resto del año es menos llamativa (7b).

❖ En las costas marinas.

1 Spotted Sandpiper

M-7 Small, active wader, breeding plumage (1a) and non-breeding plumage (1b).

❖ Widespread on sea coasts.

2 Semipalmated Plover

M-8 Small wader with distinctive collar. Breeding (2a) and non-breeding (2b) plumage.

❖ Widespread on sea coasts, sometimes at highland pools.

3 Least Sandpiper

M-6 Tiny wader with yellowish legs.

❖ Widespread on sea coasts and lagoons.

4 Grey (Black-bellied) Plover

M-6 Medium-sized wader in breeding plumage (4a) and non-breeding plumage (4b).

❖ Widespread on sea coasts and lagoons.

5 Surfbird

M-5 Small, dark sandpiper, breeding (5a) and non-breeding plumage (5b).

❖ Rocky shores.

6 Sanderling

M-8 Very active, small wader that runs rapidly along the tideline, shown in breeding (6a) and non-breeding plumage (6b).

❖ Widespread on sea coasts.

7 Ruddy Turnstone

M-8 Wader with unmistakable breeding plumage (7a) and non-breeding plumage (7b).

❖ Widespread in coastal areas.

1 Drosseluferläufer

M-7 Kleiner, aktiver Watvogel im Brutgefieder (1a) und außerhalb der Brutzeit (1b).

❖ Weit verbreitet an Meeresküsten.

2 Amerikanischer Sandregenpfeifer

M-8 Kleiner Watvogel mit ausgeprägtem Halsband. Im Brutgefieder (2a) und außerhalb der Brutzeit (2b).

❖ Weit verbreitet an Meeresküsten, manchmal auch an Tümpeln im Hochland.

3 Wiesenstrandläufer

M-6 Sehr kleiner Watvogel mit gelblichen Beinen.

❖ Weit verbreitet an Meeresküsten und Lagunen.

4 Kiebitzregenpfeifer

M-6 Mittelgroßer Watvogel im Brutgefieder (4a) und außerhalb der Brutzeit (4b).

❖ Weit verbreitet an Meeresküsten und Lagunen.

5 Gischtläufer

M-5 Kleiner, dunkler Strandläufer im Brutgefieder (5a) und außerhalb der Brutzeit (5b).

❖ Felsige Küsten.

6 Sanderling

M-8 Sehr aktiver, kleiner Watvogel, der schnell an der Hochwasserlinie entlangläuft. Im Brutgefieder (6a) und außerhalb der Brutzeit (6b).

❖ Weit verbreitet an Meeresküsten.

7 Steinwälzer

M-8 Watvogel mit unverkennbarem Brutgefieder (7a) und außerhalb der Brutzeit (7b).

❖ Weit verbreitet in Küstengebieten

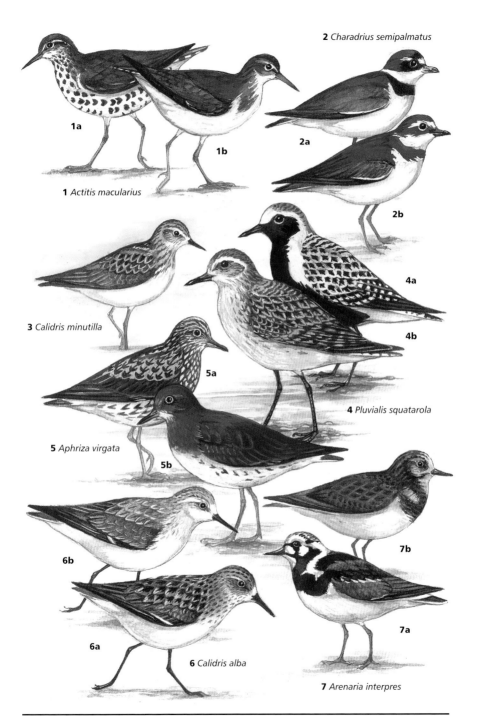

2 *Charadrius semipalmatus*

1a

1b

2a

2b

1 *Actitis macularius*

3 *Calidris minutilla*

4a

4b

5a

5 *Aphriza virgata*

4 *Pluvialis squatarola*

5b

6b

7b

6a

7a

6 *Calidris alba*

7 *Arenaria interpres*

23

1 Gavilán de Galápagos

E-3 Las hembras de este gavilán se aparean con varios machos que ayudan todos con el cuidado de las crías. Aquí pueden verse un adulto (1a) y un inmaturo (1b).

❖ Pueden encontrarse desde las costas hasta las tierras altas pero sólo anidan en las tierras bajas.

2 Aguila Pescadora

V-6 Ave de presa de gran tamaño que se alimenta sólo de peces que captura zambulléndose en el agua.

❖ Zonas costeras.

3 Halcón Peregrino

V-6 Halcón veloz que se alimenta principalmente de otras aves que captura en pleno vuelo.

❖ Acantilados marinos; muy extendido.

4 Lechuza Blanca

Se-6 Cazadora nocturna que se alimenta de ratas, ratones, insectos y pequeños pájaros.

❖ Muy extendida pero raramente visible.

5 Lechuza de Campo

Se-6 Más fácil de ver que la Lechuza Blanca, normalmente cuando vuela.

❖ Muy extendida; a veces puede verse en Genovesa donde se alimenta de las golondrinas que captura.

1 Galápagos Hawk

E-3 Females of the Galápagos hawk mate with several males, all of whom help to rear the young. Shown here are an adult (1a) and a juvenile (1b).

❖ Found from the coast to the highlands, but they breed only in the lowlands.

2 Osprey

V-6 A large raptor that feeds only on fish, which it catches by plunge-diving.

❖ Coastal areas.

3 Peregrine Falcon

V-6 A fast-flying falcon that feeds mainly on other birds, which are mainly caught in flight.

❖ Sea cliffs; widespread.

4 Barn Owl

Es-6 A nocturnal hunter that preys on rats, mice, insects, and small birds.

❖ Widespread but seldom seen.

5 Short-eared Owl

Es-6 More often seen than the Barn Owl and usually seen when flying.

❖ Widespread, often seen at Genovesa.

1 Galápagos-Bussard

E-3 Das Weibchen paart sich mit mehreren Männchen, die alle bei der Aufzucht der Jungen helfen. Hier gezeigt als Altvogel (1a) und als Jungvogel (1b).

❖ Von der Küste bis zum Hochland zu beobachten, brütet allerdings nur im Tiefland.

2 Fischadler

V-6 Ein großer Raubvogel, der sich ausschließlich von Fischen ernährt, die durch Sturztauchen gefangen werden.

❖ Küstenregionen.

3 Wanderfalke

V-6 Ein schnell fliegender Falke, der sich hauptsächlich von anderen Vögeln ernährt, welche meist im Flug erbeutet werden.

❖ Meeresfelsen, weit verbreitet.

4 Galápagos-Schleiereule

Es-6 Ein nachtaktiver Jäger, der sich von Ratten, Mäusen, Insekten und kleinen Vögeln ernährt.

❖ Weit verbreitet, aber selten zu sehen.

5 Galápagos-Sumpfohreule

Es-6 Wird häufiger gesehen als die Galápagos-Schleiereule, meist im Fluge.

❖ Weit verbreitet, häufig auf Genovesa zu sehen.

1 *Buteo galapagoensis*

1a

1b

3 *Falco peregrinus*

2 *Pandion haliaetus*

4 *Tyto alba punctatissima*

5 *Asio flammeus galapagoensis*

1 Pachay

E-4 Ave muy pequeña que pasa desapercibida y que puede volar pero apenas lo hace.

❖ Vegetación espesa y húmeda de las tierras altas.

2 Gallareta

R-5 Otra ave discreta pero de mayor tamaño que su pariente el Pachay.

❖ Vegetación espesa, principalmente en zonas agrícolas.

3 Gallareta Frentirroja (Gallinula)

R-6 Ave acuática de tamaño mediano que apenas vuela.

❖ Principalmente en las lagunas costeras.

4 Paloma de Galápagos

E-7 Esta paloma no teme a la presencia humana. Su alimentación varía, desde orugas a semillas de plantas. Las que habitan en Darwin y Wolf son subespecies separadas.

❖ Principalmente en tierras bajas y áridas.

5 Paloma Bravía

I-7 Paloma común que se encuentra en muchas ciudades alrededor del mundo.

❖ Zonas de habitación humana.

6 Cuclillo

R-7 Cuclillo tímido que pasa desapercibido y que se alimenta principalmente de insectos.

❖ En las islas más grandes.

7 Garrapatero

I-7 Ave negra, de gran tamaño, introducida por los granjeros para controlar las garrapatas del ganado y que se alimenta principalmente de saltamontes.

❖ Zonas agrícolas en las tierras altas.

1 Galápagos Rail

E-3 A very small bird that is seldom seen. It can fly but is reluctant to do so.

❖ Thick, wet vegetation in the highlands.

2 Paint-billed Crake

R-5 Another secretive bird, but larger than its relation, the Galápagos Rail.

❖ Thick vegetation mainly in the agricultural areas.

3 Moorhen (Common Gallinule)

R-6 A medium-sized waterbird that seldom flies.

❖ Mainly coastal lagoons.

4 Galápagos Dove

E-7 This dove is not afraid of people. Its food varies from caterpillars to plant seeds. Those on Darwin and Wolf are a separate subspecies.

❖ Mainly arid lowlands.

5 Rock Pigeon

I-7 Familiar dove found in many cities around the world.

❖ Areas of human habitation.

6 Dark-billed Cuckoo

R-7 Shy, seldom seen cuckoo that feeds mainly on insects.

❖ All the larger islands.

7 Smooth-billed Ani

I-7 A large black bird introduced by farmers to control cattle ticks, but it feeds mainly on grasshoppers.

❖ Agricultural areas in the highlands.

1 Galápagos-Ralle

E-4 Ein selten zu sehender, sehr kleiner Vogel. Obwohl flugfähig, fliegt er selten.

❖ Dichte, feuchte Vegetation im Hochland.

2 Goldschnabel-Sumpfhuhn

R-5 Ein weiterer scheuer Vogel, aber größer als seine Verwandte, die Galápagosralle.

❖ Dichte Vegetation, meist in der landwirtschaftlichen Zone.

3 Teichhuhn

R-6 Ein mittelgroßer Wasservogel, der selten fliegt.

❖ Hauptsächlich an Küstenlagunen.

4 Galápagos-Taube

E-7 Diese Taube hat keine Scheu vor Menschen. Sie ernährt sich von Raupen und Pflanzensamen. Die Tauben von Darwin und Wolf gehören zu einer eigenen Subspezies.

❖ Hauptsächlich im trockenen Tiefland.

5 Felsentaube

I-7 Gewöhnliche Felsentaube, wie sie in vielen Städten weltweit angetroffen wird.

❖ Menschliche Siedlungen.

6 Regenkuckuck

R-7 Scheuer, selten zu sehender Kuckuck, der sich hauptsächlich von Insekten ernährt.

❖ Auf allen größeren Inseln.

7 Glattschnabel ani

I-7 Großer, schwarzer Vogel, der von Landwirten für die Beseitigung von Kuhzecken eingeführt wurde. Er ernährt er sich aber hauptsächlich von Grashüpfern.

❖ Landwirtschaftliche Gebiete des Hochlandes.

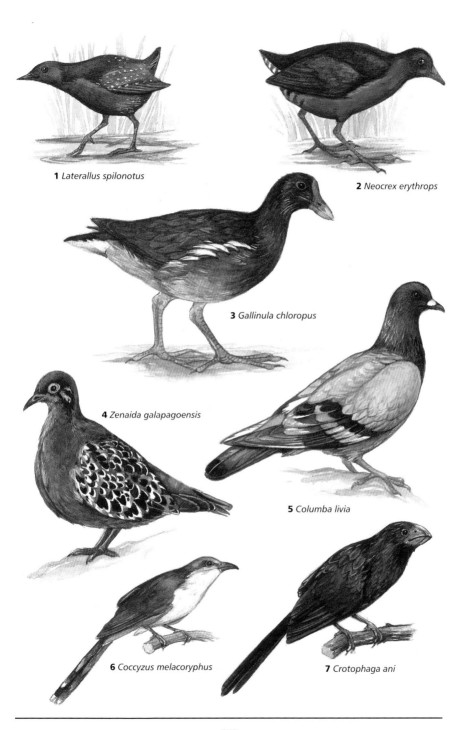

1 *Laterallus spilonotus*

2 *Neocrex erythrops*

3 *Gallinula chloropus*

4 *Zenaida galapagoensis*

5 *Columba livia*

6 *Coccyzus melacoryphus*

7 *Crotophaga ani*

27

1 Pájaro Brujo

Se-8 El macho (1a) es la única ave de color rojo brillante en Las Galápagos; (1b) es la hembra. Hay dos subspecies endémicas, P.r.nanus, que se encuentra en las islas más grandes excepto en San Cristóbal, y P.r.dubius, que se encuentra sólo en San Cristóbal.

❖ Principalmente en las tierras altas, sobre todo en Los Gemelos, en Santa Cruz.

2 Papamoscas de Galápagos

E-8 El macho y la hembra son semejantes y se parecen a la hembra del Pájaro Brujo. No temen a la presencia humana.

❖ Muy extendido en las islas principales.

3 Canario María

R-8 La única ave de color amarillo brillante en Las Galápagos. Aquí pueden verse el macho (3a) y la hembra (3b).

❖ Muy extendido en las tierras bajas y en las tierras altas.

4 Golondrina de Galápagos

E-3 Un miembro de la familia de las golondrinas, de pequeño tamaño y de color oscuro.

❖ Islas del centro y del sur, principalmente en las tierras altas.

5 Golondrina de Horquilla

M-6 Golondrina típica de cola muy bifurcada.

❖ Muy extendida.

6 Golondrina de Iglesias

M-6 El macho (6a) tiene un color uniforme azul y negro mientras que la hembra (6b) tiene el vientre más claro.

❖ Islas del sur.

1 Vermilion Flycatcher

Es-8 The male (1a) is the only bright red bird in Galápagos; (1b) is the female. There are two endemic subspecies, P.r.nanus, found on all the larger islands, except San Cristóbal, and P.r.dubius, found only on San Cristóbal.

❖ Mainly in the highlands especially at Los Gemelos on Santa Cruz.

2 Galápagos Flycatcher

E-8 Male and female similar, and resembling the female vermilion flycatcher. Unafraid of humans.

❖ Widespread on all the main islands.

3 Yellow Warbler

R-8 The only bright yellow bird in Galápagos. Male (3a) and female (3b) are shown here.

❖ Widespread in lowlands and highlands.

4 Galápagos Martin

E-3 Small, all dark-coloured member of the swallow family.

❖ Central and southern islands, mainly in highlands.

5 Barn Swallow

M-6 Typical swallow with deeply forked tail.

❖ Widespread.

6 Purple Martin

M-6 Male (6a) uniformly blue-black; female (6b) light-bellied.

❖ Southern islands.

1 Rubintyrann

Es-8 Das Männchen (1a) ist der einzige leuchtend rote Vogel auf Gal ápagos; (1b) ist das Weibchen. Es gibt zwei endemische Unterarten, P. r. nanus, die auf allen größeren Inseln außer auf San Cristóbal vorkommt, und P. r. dubius, die nur auf San Cristóbal vorkommt.

❖ Hauptsächlich im Hochland, vor allem bei Los Gemelos auf Santa Cruz.

2 Galápagos-Schopftyrann

E-8 Männchen und Weibchen sehen ähnlich aus, zu verwechseln mit dem weiblichen Rubintyrann. Hat keine Scheu vor Menschen.

❖ Weit verbreitet auf allen Hauptinseln.

3 Goldwaldsänger

R-8 Der einzige leuchtend gelbe Vogel auf Gal ápagos. Hier gezeigt sind das Männchen (3a) und das Weibchen (3b).

❖ Weit verbreitet im Tief-und Hochland.

4 Galápagos-Schwalbe

E-3 Ein kleiner, vollständig dunkel gefärbter Vertreter der Schwalben.

❖ Mittlre und südliche Inseln, hauptsächlich im Hochland.

5 Rauchschwalbe

M-6 Typische Schwalbe mit tief gegabeltem Schwanz.

❖ Weit verbreitet.

6 Purpurschwalbe

M-6 Das Männchen (6a) ist durchgehend blau-schwarz gefärbt, das Weibchen (6b) hat einen heller gefärbten Bauch.

❖ Südliche Inseln.

1b

1a

2 *Myiarchus magnirostris*

1 *Pyrocephalus rubinus*

3 *Dendroica petechia*

3a

3b

4 *Progne modesta*

5 *Hirundo rustica*

6a

6b

6 *Progne subis*

29

1 Cucuve de Galápagos

E-7 Una buena imitadora que no teme a la presencia humana. Hay seis subespecies pero no comparten territorio con ninguna otra Cucuve.

❖ Residente en la mayoría de las islas más grandes.

2 Cucuve de Española

E-3 El cucuve más grande de las Galápagos y el que tiene el pico más largo.

❖ Sólo en Española y Gardner cerca de Española.

3 Cucuve de San Cristóbal

E-2 Parecido a los otros cucuves.

❖ Sólo en San Cristóbal.

4 Cucuve de Floreana

E-1 Extinto en Floreana pero un pequeño número vive en dos isletas donde se lleva a cabo un plan de acción urgente.

❖ Sólo en Champion, cerca de Floreana y en Gardner cerca de Floreana.

5 Tordo Arrocero

M-6 Ave robusta y original que puede anidar en las islas. El plumaje del macho adulto (5a) es diferente al de la hembra y al del macho inmaturo (5b).

❖ Principalmente en las zonas agrícolas de San Cristóbal.

1 Galápagos Mockingbird

E-7 A good mimic and not afraid of humans. There are six subspecies but their ranges do not overlap those of any other species of mockingbird.

❖ Resident on most of the larger islands.

2 Española Mockingbird

E-3 The largest mockingbird in Galápagos, with the longest bill.

❖ Only on Española and Gardner-by-Española.

3 San Cristóbal Mockingbird

E-2 Similar to the other mockingbirds.

❖ Only on San Cristóbal.

4 Floreana Mockingbird

E-1 Extinct on Floreana, but small numbers live on two offshore islets where there is an emergency management plan.

❖ Only on Champion-by-Floreana and Gardner-by-Floreana.

5 Bobolink

M-6 A sturdy, distinctive bird that may be breeding. Male breeding plumage (5a) is unlike the female or the non-breeding male (5b).

❖ Mainly agricultural areas on San Cristóbal.

1 Galápagos-Spottdrossel

E-7 Ein guter Nachahmer, der keine Scheu vor Menschen hat. Es gibt sechs Unterarten und ihre Reviere überschneiden sich nicht mit denen der anderen Spottdrosseln.

❖ Auf den meisten größeren Inseln.

2 Española-Spottdrossel

E-3 Die größte Spottdrossel auf Galápagos, hat den längsten Schwanz.

❖ Kommt nur auf Españ ola und auf Gardner-by-Española vor.

3 San Cristóbal-Spottdrossel

E-2 Den anderen Spottdrosseln ähnlich.

❖ Nur auf San Cristóbal.

4 Floreana-Spottdrossel

E-1 Auf Floreana ausgestorben, aber in geringer Zahl auf den vorgelagerten, kleinen Inseln vorkommend. Ein Notfallmanagementplan zu deren Erhalt wurde entwickelt.

❖ Nur auf Champion-by-Floreana und Gardner-by-Floreana.

5 Reisstärling

M-6 Ein kräftiger, auffälliger Vogel, der manchmal auch brütet. Das Gefieder des Männchens in der Brutzeit (5a) unterscheidet sich von dem des Weibchens oder dem des nicht brütenden Männchens (5b).

❖ Hauptsächlich in den landwirtschaftlichen Gebieten auf San Cristóbal.

1 *Mimus parvulus*

3 *Mimus melanotis*

2 *Mimus macdonaldi*

5a

5b

4 *Mimus trifasciatus*

5 *Dolichonyx oryzivorus*

31

PINZONES DE DARWIN: 1

1 Pinzón Terrestre de Pico Agudo

E-7 Existen tres subespecies pero las poblaciones raramente comparten territorio; las de Darwin y Wolf suelen alimentarse de la sangre de los piqueros blancos por lo que se les llama pinzones vampiros.

❖ Por todas partes en las islas más grandes.

2 Gran Pinzón Terrestre

E-6 El mayor de los pinzones terrestres, con un pico muy grande; a menudo solitario.

❖ Orillas y zonas áridas.

3 Pequeño Pinzón Terrestre

E-9 El más pequeño de los pinzones terrestres, con un pico corto; a menudo se alimenta de los parásitos de la piel de los reptiles.

❖ Muy extendido.

4 Mediano Pinzón Terrestre

E-9 Pinzón de tamaño intermedio; el tamaño del pico varía.

❖ Muy extendido; a menudo se le ve en bandadas en compañia del pequeño pinzón terrestre.

5 Gran Pinzón de Cacto

E-7 Existen tres subespecies de este pinzón que a menudo se alimenta en el suelo.

❖ Española, Genovesa, Darwin y Wolf. En orillas y zonas áridas.

6 Pinzón de Cacto

E-7 Existen cuatro subespecies de este pinzón que anida en el cactus Opuntia.

❖ En orillas y zonas áridas.

DARWIN'S FINCHES: 1

1 Sharp-beaked Ground Finch

E-7 There are three subspecies, but the populations seldom overlap; those on Darwin and Wolf often feed on the blood of Nazca boobies, and are called vampire finches. Shown here are male (1a) and female (1b).

❖ Larger islands, all zones.

2 Large Ground Finch

E-6 The largest ground finch with very large beak; often solitary.

❖ Shore and Arid zones.

3 Small Ground Finch

E-9 Smallest ground finch with a short beak; it often feeds on parasites on the skin of reptiles.

❖ Widespread in all zones.

4 Medium Ground Finch

E-9 Intermediate in size, as its name suggests; beak size is variable.

❖ Widespread in most zones, often in flocks with small ground finches.

5 Large Cactus Finch

E-7 Three subspecies. This bird often feeds on the ground.

❖ Española, Genovesa, Darwin and Wolf, in Shore and Arid zones.

6 Cactus Finch

E-7 There are four subspecies of this finch, which nests in the Opuntia cactus.

❖ Shore and Arid zones.

DARWINS FINKEN: 1

1 Spitzschnabel-Grundfink

E-7 Es gibt drei Unterarten aber deren Populationen überschneiden sich nur selten. Jene auf Darwin und Wolf ernähren sich oft von dem Blut der Nazca-Tölpel und werden daher auch Vampirfinken genannt.

❖ Alle Gebiete der größeren Inseln.

2 Großer Grundfink

E-6 Der größte der Grundfink en, hat einen sehr großen Schnabel; häufig Einzelgänger.

❖ Küsten-und Trockengebiete.

3 Kleiner Grundfink

E-9 Der kleinste der Grundfink en, hat einen kurzen Schnabel; ernährt sich häufig von Hautparasiten auf Reptilien.

❖ Weit verbreitet in allen Gebieten.

4 Mittlerer Grundfink

E-9 Von mittlerer Größe, wie der Name besagt; Schnabelgröße variiert.

❖ Weit verbreitet in den meisten Gebieten, oft in Schwärmen mit dem Kleinen Grundfink.

5 Großer Kaktusfink

E-7 Drei Unterarten. Dieser Vogel frisst oft am Boden.

❖ Española, Genovesa, Darwin und Wolf, in Küsten-und Trockengebieten.

6 Kaktus-Grundfink

E-7 sbt vier Unterarten von dieser Finkenart; brütet in Opuntia-Kakteen.

❖ Küsten-und Trockengebiete.

1 *Geospiza difficilis*

1a

1b

2 *Geospiza magnirostris*

3 *Geospiza fuliginosa*

4 *Geospiza fortis*

5 *Geospiza conirostris*

6 *Geospiza scandens*

PINZONES DE DARWIN: 2

1 Pinzón Vegetariano

E-6 Pinzón grande que se mueve en silencio al comer. Su canto es muy musical.

❖ En las islas grandes.

2 Pequeño Pinzón Arbóreo

E-8 El más pequeño de los pinzones arbóreos se cuelga boca abajo de las ramas mientras come. Macho (2a) y hembra (2b).

❖ Muy extendido en las islas más grandes.

3 Gran Pinzón Arbóreo

E-6 El mayor de los pinzones arbóreos. La punta superior del pico es como la del loro y sobresale por encima de la otra.

❖ Anida principalmente en las tierras altas de las islas grandes.

4 Mediano Pinzón Arbóreo

E-1 Distribución restringida.

❖ Se encuentra sólo en Floreana y principalmente en las tierras altas.

5 Pinzón Cantor

E-8 El menor de los pinzones de Darwin. Hay ocho subespecies con plumaje de colores variados.

❖ Muy extendido.

6 Pinzón Carpintero

E-7 Utiliza ramitas o espinas de cactus para extraer las larvas de la madera podrida.

❖ De las zonas áridas a las húmedas.

7 Pinzón de Manglar

E-1 De comportamiento semejante al del pinzón carpintero. Quizá haya menos de 40 parejas.

❖ Manglares del noroeste de Isabela.

DARWIN'S FINCHES: 2

1 Vegetarian Finch

E-6 A large finch that moves quietly when feeding; it has a musical song.

❖ Mainly in the larger islands.

2 Small Tree Finch

E-8 The smallest tree finch sometimes hangs upside down from branches while feeding. Male (2a) and female (2b).

❖ Widespread in the larger islands.

3 Large Tree Finch

E-6 Largest of the tree finches. The tips of its parrot-like beak overlap.

❖ Breeds mainly in highlands of larger islands.

4 Medium Tree Finch

E-1 Restricted distribution.

❖ Only in Floreana, and mainly in the highlands.

5 Warbler Finch

E-8 The smallest of the Darwin's finches with variable plumage colours.

❖ Widespread, from Arid zone to highlands.

6 Woodpecker Finch

E-7 This bird uses twigs or cactus spines to extract larvae from rotten wood.

❖ From Arid to Humid zones.

7 Mangrove Finch

E-1 Similar behaviour to Woodpecker Finch. Maybe fewer than 40 pairs.

❖ Mangroves of north-western Isabela.

DARWINS FINKEN: 2 .

1 Dickschnabel-Darwinfink

E-6 Ein großer Fink, der sich beim Fressen leise bewegt. Hat einen musikalischen Gesang.

❖ Hauptsächlich auf größeren Inseln.

2 Kleiner Baumfink

E-8 Der kleinste der Baumfinken. Frisst manchmal kopfüber von Zweigen hängend. Männchen (2a) und Weibchen (2b).

❖ Weit verbreitet auf den größeren Inseln.

3 Großer Baumfink

E-6 Der größte der Baumfinken. Die Spitzen des papageienförmigen Schnabels überkreuzen sich.

❖ Brütet meist im Hochland der größeren Inseln.

4 Mittlerer Baumfink

E-1 Eingeschränkte Verbreitung.

❖ Nur auf Floreana, meist im Hochland.

5 Waldsängerfink (auch Laubsängerfink)

E-8 Kleinster Darwinfink mit verschieden gefärbtem Gefieder.

❖ Weit verbreitet, vom Trockengebiet zum Hochland.

6 Spechtfink

E-7 Dieser Fink benutzt Zweige oder Kaktusstacheln, um Larven aus verrottetem Holz zu holen.

❖ Von Trocken- bis Feuchtgebieten.

7 Mangrovenfink

E-1 Verhalten ähnlich dem des Spechtfinks. Wahrscheinlich weniger als 40 Brutpaare.

❖ Mangroven im Nordwesten von Isabela.

1 *Platyspiza crassirostris*

2 *Camarhynchus parvulus*

2a

2b

4 *Camarhynchus pauper*

3 *Camarhynchus psittacula*

5 *Certhidea olivacea*

6 *Camarhynchus pallidus*

7 *Camarhynchus heliobates*

PINZONES DE DARWIN: 3

Comparación de los picos

Estas pequeñas aves tuvieron una gran influencia sobre Charles Darwin cuando este trabajaba sobre la teoría de la evolución. El tamaño y la forma de sus picos están altamente relacionados con las diferentes fuentes de alimentos de las que se nutren. A los largo de muchos años os científicos los han estudiado con detalle y han sido capaces de detectar su evolución en "tiempo real".

1 **Pinzón Terrestre de Pico Agudo .**

2 **Pinzón de Cacto**

3 **Gran Pinzón de Cacto**

4 **Gran Pinzón Terrestre**

5 **Mediano Pinzón Terrestre**

6 **Pequeño Pinzón Terrestre**

7 **Pinzón Cantor**

8 **Pequeño Pinzón Arbóreo**

9 **Mediano Pinzón Arbóreo**

10 **Gran Pinzón Arbóreo**

11 **Pinzón Vegetariano**

12 **Pinzón de Manglar**

13 **Pinzón Carpintero**

DARWIN'S FINCHES: 3

A comparison of their beaks.

These small birds had a great influence on Charles Darwin as he worked on his theory of evolution. The size and shape of their beaks are closely related to their different food sources. Scientists have made detailed studies of them over many years and have been able to detect evolution "in real time".

1 **Sharp-beaked Ground Finch**

2 **Cactus Finch**

3 **Large Cactus Finch**

4 **Large Ground Finch**

5 **Medium Ground Finch**

6 **Small Ground Finch**

7 **Warbler Finch**

8 **Small Tree Finch**

9 **Medium Tree Finch**

10 **Large Tree Finch**

11 **Vegetarian Finch**

12 **Mangrove Finch**

13 **Woodpecker Finch**

DARWINS FINKEN: 3

Ein Vergleich der Schnäbel

Diese kleinen Vögel hatten einen bedeutenden Einfluss auf Charles Darwin, während er an seiner Evolutionstheorie arbeitete. Größe und Form der Schnäbel sind eng mit der Art ihrer Nahrung verbunden. Wissenschaftler haben über Jahre hinweg detaillierte Untersuchungen an den Schnäbeln durchgeführt und konnten dadurch Evolution in "Echtzeit" nachweisen.

1 **Spitzschnabel-Grundfink**

2 **Kaktus-Grundfink**

3 **Großer Kaktusfink**

4 **Spitzschnabel-Grundfink**

5 **Mittlerer Grundfink**

6 **Kleiner Grundfink**

7 **Waldsängerfink**

8 **Kleiner Baumfink**

9 **Mittlerer Baumfink**

10 **Großer Baumfink**

11 **Dickschnabel-Darwinfink**

12 **Mangrovenfink**

13 **Spechtfink**

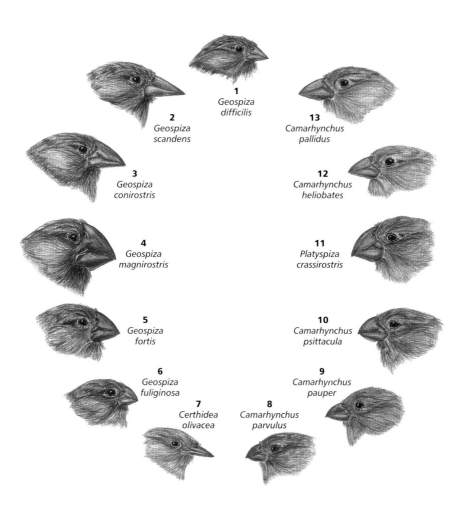

1
*Geospiza
difficilis*

2
*Geospiza
scandens*

3
*Geospiza
conirostris*

4
*Geospiza
magnirostris*

5
*Geospiza
fortis*

6
*Geospiza
fuliginosa*

7
*Certhidea
olivacea*

8
*Camarhynchus
parvulus*

9
*Camarhynchus
pauper*

10
*Camarhynchus
psittacula*

11
*Platyspiza
crassirostris*

12
*Camarhynchus
heliobates*

13
*Camarhynchus
pallidus*

MAMÍFEROS TERRESTRES

LAND MAMMALS

LANDSÄUGETIERE

1 Rata Grande de Fernandina

E-3 Poco se sabe de esta especie de rata de patas blancas que desarrolla su actividad por la noche.

❖ Sólo en Fernandina, pero extendida por toda la isla.

2 Rata Pequeña de Fernandina

E-3 No se sabe nada de esta especie de patas oscuras descubierta en 1995.

❖ Sólo en Fernandina.

3 Rata de Santiago

E-3 Redescubierta en 1997, ésta es la única de estos roedores que puede competir con la rata negra.

❖ Sólo en Santiago, en el norte de la isla.

4 Rata Endémica de Galápagos

E-3 Esta rata no teme al hombre y desarrolla su actividad por la noche.

❖ Sólo en Santa Fé, especialmente en la zona árida.

5 Murciélago Escarchado

Se-7 Un murciélago de gran tamaño que vuela rápido y por encima de los ocho metros.

❖ Está muy extendido y se posa para pasar la noche en árboles y cuevas.

6 Murciélago Vespertino Galápagueño

Se-7 Un murciélago de menor tamaño y de vuelo más bajo que se encuentra en las tierras altas y bajas.

❖ Santa Cruz, San Cristóbal.

1 Large Fernandina Mouse

E-3 Little is known about this species with white feet, which is active at night.

❖ Only on Fernandina, but in all parts of the island.

2 Small Fernandina Mouse

E-3 Nothing is known about this species with dark feet, discovered in 1995.

❖ Only on Fernandina.

3 Santiago Mouse

E-3 Rediscovered in 1997, and the only one of these rodents that can compete with the black rat.

❖ Only on Santiago, in the north of the island.

4 Galápagos Rice Rat

E-3 Active at night, and unafraid of humans.

❖ Only on Santa Fé, especially in the Arid zone.

5 Hoary Bat

Es-7 A large, fast-flying bat that flies at 8m or above.

❖ Widespread. and roosts in trees and caves.

6 Galápagos Red Bat

Es-7 A smallish, low-flying bat. found in the highlands and lowlands.

❖ Santa Cruz, San Cristóbal.

1 Große Fernandina-Maus

E-3 Es gibt nur wenig Information über diese weißfüßige, nachtaktive Art.

❖ Nur auf Fernandina, aber in allen Teilen der Insel.

2 Kleine Fernandina-Maus

E-3 Es gibt keine Information über diese dunkelfüßige Art, die 1995 entdeckt wurde.

❖ Nur auf Fernandina.

3 Santiago-Maus

E-3 Wurde 1997 wieder entdeckt und ist die einzige der diese Nagetiere die mit der schwarzen Hausratte konkurrieren kann.

❖ Nur auf Santiago, im Norden der Insel.

4 Galápagos-Reisratte

E-3 Nachtaktiv und ohne Scheu vor Menschen.

❖ Nur auf Santa Fé, besonders in der Trockenzone.

5 Eisgraue Fledermaus

Es-7 Eine große, schnell fliegende Fledermaus, die über 8 m hoch fliegt.

❖ Weit verbreitet, schlafen in Bäumen und Höhlen.

6 Galápagos-Fledermaus

Es-7 Eine kleine, niedrig fliegende Fledermaus, die im Hoch-und Flachland anzutreffen ist.

❖ Santa Cruz, San Cristóbal

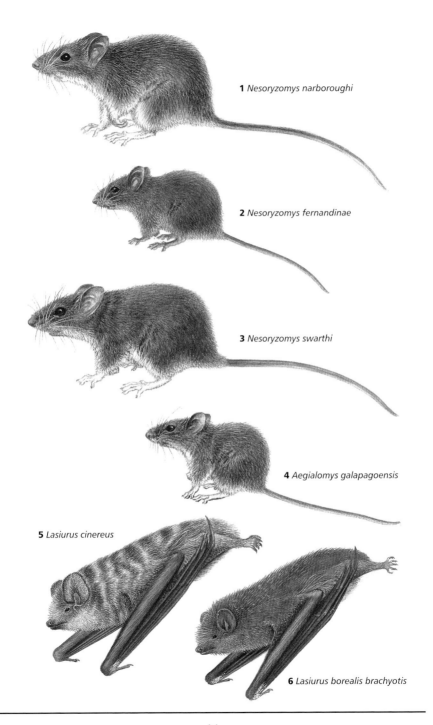

1 *Nesoryzomys narboroughi*

2 *Nesoryzomys fernandinae*

3 *Nesoryzomys swarthi*

4 *Aegialomys galapagoensis*

5 *Lasiurus cinereus*

6 *Lasiurus borealis brachyotis*

MAMÍFEROS MARINOS

MARINE MAMMALS

MEERESSÄUGETIERE

1 Lobo Marino de Galápagos

Se-8 Un pariente local del Lobo Marino de California que forma grandes colonias en las playas arenosas. El macho es mucho más grande que la hembra y puede ser peligroso en temporada de cría. Los jóvenes son a menudo muy amistosos y juegan en el agua con buceadores y submarinistas. Se alimentan durante el día.

❖ Extendido en las costas marinas.

2 Lobo Peletero de Galápagos

E-7 Es mucho más pequeño que el León Marino y tiene el pelaje más espeso, pero aparte de eso tiene una apariencia muy similar. Forman pequeñas colonias en las orillas rocosas y a veces son difíciles de ver porque prefieren dormir a la sombra de las rocas en las horas de más calor. Se alimentan por la noche.

❖ Costas rocosas.

1 Galápagos Sea Lion

Es-2 A local relative of the California Sea Lion that forms large colonies on sandy beaches. The male is much larger than the female, and can be dangerous in the breeding season. The young seals are often very friendly and playful in the water with divers and snorkellers. They feed during the day.

❖ Widespread on sea coasts.

2 Galápagos Fur Seal

E-2 Much smaller than the Sea Lion, and with thicker fur, but otherwise quite similar in appearance. They form small colonies on rocky shores, and are sometimes difficult to see as they prefer to sleep in the shade of rocks during the heat of the day. They feed at night.

❖ Rocky coasts.

1 Galápagos-Seelöwe

Es-2 Verwandter des Kalifornischen Seelöwen, der große Kolonien an sandigen Stränden aus bildet. Das Männchen ist sehr viel größer als das Weibchen und kann während der Brutzeit gefährlich werden. Die jungen Seelöwen sind häufig sehr freundlich und spielen mit Tauchern und Schnorchlern im Wasser. Seelöwen fressen am Tage.

❖ Weit verbreitet an Meeresküsten.

2 Galápagos-Seebär (auch Galápagos-Robbe).

E-2 Sehr viel kleiner als der Galápagos-Seelöwe, mit einem dichteren Fell, aber ansonsten diesem sehr ähnlich. Sie leben in kleinen Kolonien an felsigen Küsten und sind teilweise schwer zu sehen, da sie in der Mittagshitze meist im Schatten der Felsen schlafen. Seebären fressen nachts.

❖ Felsige Küsten.

1 *Zalophus californianus*

2 *Arctocephalus galapagoensis*

1 Ballena Minke

5 La más pequeña de los rorcuales; se alimenta de peces y de pequeños crustáces conocidos como krill.

❖ Mar adentro, pero apenas se ve.

2 Ballena Sei

2 Una gran ballena que emite al respirar un chorro de agua alto y estrcho. A menudo presenta cicatrices en las aletas. Se alimenta de calamares, de peces y de pequeños crustáces conocidos como krill.

❖ Mar adentro, pero apenas se ve.

3 Ballena de Bryde

7 Es parecida a la Ballena Sei pero con tres crestas longitudinales en la cabeza. Se alimenta de peces.

❖ Puede verse bastante a menudo, cerca de la orilla y mar adentro.

4 Ballena Azul

2 El animal más grande del mundo, que emite al respirar un chorro de agua que puede alcanzar los 10 metros. Se alimenta de pequeños crustáces conocidos como krill.

❖ Mar adentro.

5 Ballena Jorobada

5 Esta ballena salta a menudo fuera del agua y sus grandes aletas parecen alas.

❖ Cerca de la orilla y mar adentro.

6 Cachalote

3 El mayor cetáceo dentado; se alimenta de calamares. El chorro que emite al respirar se inclina hacia adelante y hacia la izquierda.

❖ Mar adentro.

1 Minke Whale

5 The smallest of the baleen whales, it feeds on krill and fish.

❖ Offshore, but seldom seen.

2 Sei Whale

2 A large whale with a tall, thin "blow". It often has pale scars on its sides. It feeds on krill, fish, and squid.

❖ Offshore, but seldom seen.

3 Bryde's Whale

7 Similar to Sei Whale but with three ridges on top of its head. It prefers to eat fish.

❖ Seen fairly often, inshore and offshore.

4 Blue Whale

2 The largest animal in the world, its "blow" may be 10 m high. It feeds on krill.

❖ Offshore.

5 Humpback Whale

5 This whale breaches (jumps out of the water) quite often. Its large flippers look like wings.

❖ Inshore and offshore.

6 Sperm Whale

3 The largest toothed whale, it feeds on squid. The "blow" is angled forward and to the left.

❖ Offshore.

1 Nördlicher Zwergwal

5 Der kleinste der Bartenwale, ernährt sich von Krill und Fischen.

❖ Offenes Meer, aber selten zu sehen.

2 Seiwal

5 Ein großer Wal, mit einem langen, dünnen Blas. Er hat oftmals helle Narben an den Flanken. Ernährt sich von Krill, Fischen und Tintenfischen.

❖ Offenes Meer, aber selten zu sehen.

3 Brydewal

7 Ähnlich dem Seiwal, aber mit drei Furchen auf dem Kopf. Ernährt sich meist von Fischen.

❖ Relativ häufig zu sehen, küstennah und im offenen Meer.

4 Blauwal

2 Das größte Tier der Welt, sein Blas erreicht eine Höhe von 10 m. Ernährt sich von Krill.

❖ Offenes Meer.

5 Buckelwal

3 Dieser Wal taucht oft aus dem Wasser auf. Seine großen Flipper sehen aus wie Flügel.

❖ Küstennah und offenes Meer.

6 Pottwal

3 Der größte Zahnwal, ernährt sich von Tintenfischen. Der Blas ist nach vorne links gerichtet.

❖ Offenes Meer.

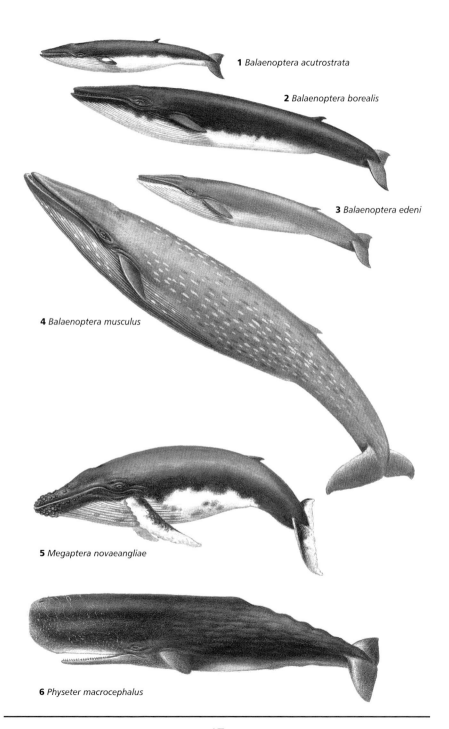

1 *Balaenoptera acutrostrata*

2 *Balaenoptera borealis*

3 *Balaenoptera edeni*

4 *Balaenoptera musculus*

5 *Megaptera novaeangliae*

6 *Physeter macrocephalus*

1 Orca

7 Un poderoso predador con una aleta dorsal que puede alcanzar los dos metros. A menudo ataca a otros mamíferos marinos.

❖ Alta mar y cerca de la orilla.

2 Ballena Piloto

6 Esta ballena, con una característica cabeza redondeada, se alimenta de calamares.

❖ Alta mar y cerca de la orilla.

3 Falsa Orca

6 De color oscuro uniforme, se alimentan de calamares y peces y a menudo salen a la superficie.

❖ Alta mar y cerca de la orilla.

4 Zifio Común

6 Esta ballena, de color marrón claro, se alimenta de calamares y peces.

❖ Alta mar.

5 Delfín Mular

7 El delfín más común en Las Galápagos. Es un animal social al que le gusta seguir las estelas de los barcos.

❖ Alta mar y cerca de la orilla.

6 Delfín Gris

6 Un delfín de color pálido que prefiere las aguas profundas y se alimenta de calamares. Los adultos tienen a menudo heridas y cicatrices provocadas por las peleas contra sus presas.

❖ Alta mar.

7 Delfín Común

7 Este delfín, pequeño y ágil, tiene la parte inferior de color crema y nada en grupos muy grandes.

❖ Principalmente en alta mar.

1 Orca (Killer Whale)

7 A powerful predator with a tall dorsal fin, that may reach 2 m. It often attacks other marine mammals.

❖ Offshore and inshore.

2 Short-finned Pilot Whale

6 This whale has a distinctive, rounded head. It feeds on squid.

❖ Offshore and inshore.

3 False Killer Whale

6 Uniformly dark in colour, they feed on fish and squid, and are often active on the surface.

❖ Offshore and inshore.

4 Cuvier's Beaked Whale

6 This whale is pale brown in colour and feeds on squid and fish.

❖ Mostly offshore.

5 Bottle-nose Dolphin

7 The dolphin most seen in Galápagos. A social animal that likes to ride the bow-waves of boats.

❖ Often close to shore.

6 Risso's Dolphin

6 A pale-coloured dolphin that prefers deep water. Adults are scarred by squids, their prey.

❖ Offshore.

7 Short-beaked Common Dolphin

7 This small, agile dolphin has a cream-coloured under-side. It swims in very large groups.

❖ Mainly offshore.

1 Großer Schwertwal (auch Orca)

7 Ein kräftiger Räuber, mit einer großen Rückenflosse, die 2 m lang sein kann. Er greift häufig andere Meeressäugetiere an.

❖ Offenes Meer und Küstennähe.

2 Kurzflossen-Grindwal

6 Dieser Wal hat einen markanten, runden Kopf. Er ernährt sich von Tintenfischen.

❖ Offenes Meer und Küstennähe.

3 Kleiner Schwertwal (auch Falscher Orca)

6 Hat eine einheitlich dunkle Färbung und ernährt sich von Fischen und Tintenfischen. Bewegt sich häufig an der Wasseroberfläche.

❖ Offenes Meer und Küstennähe.

4 Cuvier-Schnabelwal

6 Dieser Wal ist hellbraun gefärbt und ernährt sich von Fischen und Tintenfischen.

❖ Meist im offenen Meer.

5 Großer Tümmler

7 Der auf Galápagos am häufigsten zu beobachtende Delfin. Ein sehr soziales Tier, das gerne in der Bugwelle von Schiffen mitschwimmt.

❖ Oftmals in Küstennähe.

6 Rundkopfdelfin (auch Rissos-Delfin)

6 Ein hell gefärbter Delfin, der das tiefe Gewässer bevorzugt. Erwachsene Tiere tragen Narben von ihren Beutetieren, den Tintenfischen.

❖ Offenes Meer.

7 Gemeiner (Gewöhnlicher) Delfin

7 Dieser kleine, flinke Delfin hat eine cremefarbene Unterseite. Er schwimmt in sehr großen Gruppen.

❖ Meist im offenen Meer.

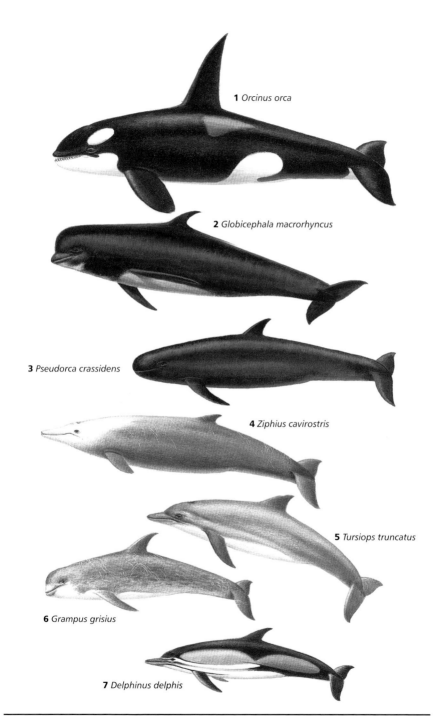

1 *Orcinus orca*

2 *Globicephala macrorhyncus*

3 *Pseudorca crassidens*

4 *Ziphius cavirostris*

5 *Tursiops truncatus*

6 *Grampus grisius*

7 *Delphinus delphis*

REPTILES

REPTILES

REPTILIEN

1 Tortuga Gigante de las Galápagos

E-3 En las islas Galápagos todavía sobreviven once subespecies de esta tortuga. Los dos tipos principales son las que tienen el caparazón en forma de cúpula (1a) y las que lo tienen en forma de silla de montar (1b). La palabra galápago deriva de un antiguo vocablo español que significa silla de montar.

❖ El mejor lugar para ver a estas tortugas en su hábitat natural es la isla de Santa Cruz; también pueden verse en cautividad, en la misma isla, en la Estación Científica Charles Darwin, donde puede verse normalmente a "Lonesome George" (1c), la última superviviente de las subespecies de la isla Pinta.

2 Tortuga Verde

R-2 Estos reptiles marinos salen a la orilla a poner los huevos, de Diciembre a Junio. El color de sus caparazones varía de verde oscuro a negro.

❖ Playas arenosas, especialmente en Punta Cormorán en la isla Floreana y Bartolomé.

3 Tortuga Carey

M-1 Una pequeña tortuga que visita las islas de forma regular. De ella se obtiene la concha de carey.

❖ Costas marinas.

1 Galápagos Giant Tortoise

E-3 Eleven subspecies still survive in Galápagos. The two main types have carapaces (shells) that are dome-shaped (1a) or saddle-backed (1b). The word galápago is an old Spanish name for a saddle.

❖ The best place to see these tortoises in the wild is Santa Cruz Island; they can also be seen in captivity on the same island at the Charles Darwin Research Station. Here it is usually possible to see "Lonesome George" (1c), the last survivor of the Pinta Island subspecies.

2 Green Turtle

R-2 These marine reptiles come ashore to lay eggs, from December to June. Their carapaces vary in colour from dark green to black.

❖ Sandy beaches, especially at Punta Cormarán on Floreana Island, and Bartolomé.

3 Hawksbill Turtle

M-1 A small turtle that is a regular visitor, and is the original source of "tortoiseshell".

❖ Sea coasts.

1 Galápagos-Riesenschildkröte

E-3 Es leben noch elf Unterarten auf Galápagos. Die beiden Hauptunterarten haben entweder einen kuppelförmigen (1a) oder einen sattelförmigen (1b) Panzer. Das Wort galápago ist ein alter spanischer Begriff für einen Sattel.

❖ Die Insel Santa Cruz ist der beste Ort, um Schildkröten in freier Wildbahn zu sehen; an der Charles Darwin Forschungsstation können sie auch in Gefangenschaft beobachtet werden. Hier ist es normalerweise möglich, „Lonesome George" (1c) zu sehen, den letzten Überlebenden der Unterart der Insel Pinta.

2 Grüne Meeresschildkröte (auch Suppenschildkröte)

R-2 Diese Meeresreptilie schwimmt an Land, um von Dezember bis Juni dort ihre Eier abzulegen. Die Farbe ihres Panzers variiert von dunkelgrün bis schwarz.

❖ Sandige Strände, vor allem bei Punta Cormorán auf der Insel Floreana und auf Bartolomé.

3 Echte Karettschildkröte

M-1 Diese kleine Meeresschildkröte ist ein häufiger Gast und aus ihrem Panzer wurde früher „Schildpatt" hergestellt.

❖ Meeresküsten.

1a

1b

1 *Chelonoidis nigra*

1c

2 *Chelonia mydas agassizi*

3 *Eretmochelys imbricata*

1 Serpiente de Española
E-7.

❖ En Española y en Gardner.

2 Serpiente de Isabela.
E-7.

❖ En Isabela y en Fernandina.

3 Serpiente de Steindachner
E-7.

❖ En Santa Cruz, en Santiago y en Rábida.

4 Serpiente de Floreana variedad rayada
E-7.

❖ En Floreana y en San Cristóbal.

5 Serpiente de Floreana variedad manchada
E-7.

❖ En Floreana y en San Cristóbal.

La situación de las serpientes de las islas Galápagos todavía no es muy conocida, pero esperamos ofrecer más información al respecto en una futura edición. Como todas las serpientes, éstas cazan estrangulando a sus presas por medio de la constricción.

1 Española Snake
E-7.

❖ Española, Gardner.

2 Isabela Snake
E-7.

❖ Isabela, Fernandina.

3 Steindachner's Snake
E-7.

❖ Santa Cruz, Santiago, Rabida.

4 Floreana Snake striped form
E-7.

❖ Floreana, San Cristóbal.

5 Floreana Snake spotted form
E-7.

❖ Floreana, San Cristóbal.

The status of the Galápagos snakes is not well known, but we hope to provide more information in a future edition. Like all snakes, these catch their prey by constriction.

1 Española-Schlange
E-7.

❖ Española, Gardner.

2 Isabela-Schlange
E-7.

❖ Isabela, Fernandina.

3 Steindachner-Schlange
E-7.

❖ Santa Cruz, Santiago, Rábida.

4 Floreana-Schlange gestreifte Form
E-7.

❖ Floreana, San Cristóbal.

5 Floreana-Schlange gefleckte Form
E-7.

❖ Floreana, San Cristóbal.

Über den Status der Galápagos-Schlangen ist bislang wenig bekannt, aber wir hoffen, in der nächsten Auflage mehr Information darüber geben zu können. Alle Schlangen fangen ihre Beute durch einen Würgegriff.

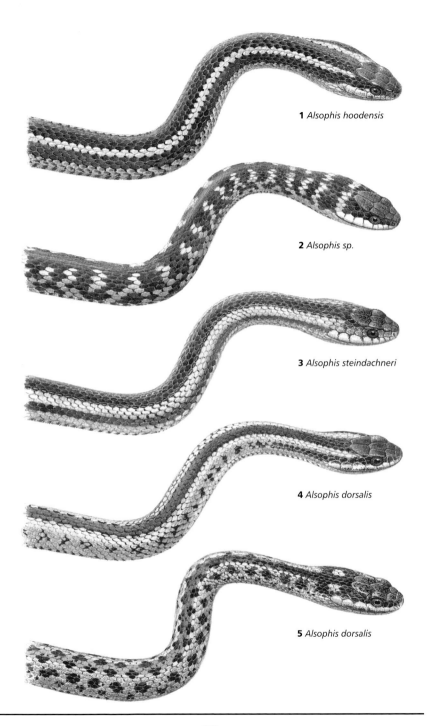

1 *Alsophis hoodensis*

2 *Alsophis sp.*

3 *Alsophis steindachneri*

4 *Alsophis dorsalis*

5 *Alsophis dorsalis*

1 Lagartija de lava de Galápagos

E-7 Bastante común en las tierras bajas de diez de las islas. Los machos y las hembras exhiben colores muy diferentes.

❖ Santa Fé, Santa Cruz, Plaza Sur, Baltra, Seymour Norte, Daphne Mayor, Santiago, Rábida, Isabela y Fernandina.

2 Lagartija de lava de Española

E-7 El ejemplar más grande de la especie de lagartija de lava llega a medir 30 cm de longitud.

❖ Se encuentra sólo en Española.

3 Lagartija de lava de San Cristóbal

E-7.

❖ Se encuentra sólo en San Cristóbal.

Hay otras cuatro especies de lagartija de lava en las islas Galápagos, en las islas de Marchena, Pinta, Pinzón y Floreana. La especie de Floreana es la más pequeña del archipiélago (mide alrededor de 15cm de longitud).

1 Galápagos Lava Lizard

E-7 Fairly common in the lowland areas of ten islands. Males and females have very different colours.

❖ Santa Fé, Santa Cruz, Plaza Sur, Baltra, Seymour Norte, Daphne Mayor, Santiago, Rábida, Isabela, & Fernandina.

2 Española Lava Lizard

E-7 The largest of the lava lizard species at up to 30cm in length.

❖ Found only on Española.

3 San Cristóbal Lava Lizard

E-7.

❖ Found only on San Cristóbal.

There are four other species of lava lizard in Galápagos, found on the islands of Marchena, Pinta, Pinzón, and Floreana. The Floreana species is the smallest in the archipelago (about 15 cm in length).

1 Galápagos-Lavaechse

E-7 Kommt recht häufig im Tiefland von zehn Inseln vor. Männchen und Weibchen sind sehr unterschiedlich gefärbt.

❖ Santa Fé, Santa Cruz, Plaza Sur, Baltra, Seymour Norte, Daphne Mayor, Santiago, Rábida, Isabela, & Fernandina.

2 Española-Lavaechse

E-7 Die größte der Lavaechsen, mit einer Länge von bis zu 30 cm.

❖ Nur auf Española.

3 San Cristóbal-Lavaechse

E-7.

❖ Nur auf San Cristóbal.

Es gibt noch vier weitere Lavaechsenarten auf Galápagos, die auf Marchena, Pinta, Pinzón und Floreana vorkommen. Die Floreana-Lavaechse ist die kleinste im Archipel (mit einer Länge von etwa 15 cm).

.

1 *Tropidurus albemarlensis*

2 *Tropidurus delanonis*

3 *Tropidurus bivattatus*

Existen nueve especies de salamanquesas y gecos en las islas Galápagos. Estos pequeños reptiles nocturnos comen insectos y son capaces de trepar por las paredes e incluso de andar por el techo de los edificios.

1 Gonatodes caudiscutatus

I-7 Este geco, que proviene originariamente de la zona interior de Ecuador, es bastante común en zonas habitadas.

❖ San Cristóbal.

2 Phyllodactylus reissi

I-7 Este reptil, originario de las costas ecuatorianas, es nuevo en las islas Galápagos y es mucho má grande que cualquiera de las especies endémicas.

❖ Zonas habitadas de Santa Cruz.

3 Lepidodactylus lugrubris

I-7 Este geco era, en su origen, nativo del sureste asiático.

❖ Zonas habitadas de San Cristóbal y Santa Cruz.

4 Phyllodactylus galapagoensis

E-7 El geco de dedos hojiformes de Galápagos es una especie endémica de colorido muy variable.

❖ Santa Cruz, Daphne Major, Pinzón, Santiago, Isabela y Fernandina.

5 Phyllodactylus bauri

E-7 Geco de dedos hojiformes de Baur.

❖ Española y Floreana.

Hay otras especies endémicas de gecos en Santa Fé y Wolf, y dos más en San Cristóbal, que no aparecen ilustradas.

There are nine species of Geckos in Galápagos. These small nocturnal reptiles eat insects and are able to climb walls and even walk on the ceiling of buildings.

1 Shieldhead Gecko

I-7 Originally from mainland Ecuador, this gecko is fairly common in inhabited areas.

❖ San Cristóbal.

2 Phyllodactylus reissi

I-7 A native of coastal Ecuador, this newcomer is much larger than any of the endemic species.

❖ Inhabited areas of Santa Cruz.

3 Lepidodactylus lugrubris

I-7 This gecko was originally a native of South-East Asia.

❖ Inhabited areas of San Cristóbal and Santa Cruz.

4 Galápagos Leaf-toed Gecko

E-7 An endemic species with very variable colouring.

❖ Santa Cruz, Daphne Major, Pinzón, Santiago, Isabela, and Fernandina.

5 Baur's Leaf-toed Gecko

E-7.

❖ Española and Floreana.

Not illustrated are endemic gecko species on Santa Fé and Wolf, as well as two more on San Cristóbal.

Es gibt auf Galápagos neun Geckoarten. Diese kleinen nachtaktiven Reptilien ernähren sich von Insekten und können Wände und sogar Zimmerdecken entlang laufen.

1 Gonatodes caudiscutatus

I-7 Dieser Gecko kommt ursprünglich vom ecuadorianischen Festland und ist häufig in bewohnten Gebieten anzutreffen.

❖ San Cristóbal.

2 Peruanischer Blattfingergecko

I-7 Dieser von der Küste Ecuadors stammende Neuankömmling ist sehr viel größer als die endemischen Arten.

❖ Bewohnte Gebiete auf Santa Cruz.

3 Lepidodactylus lugrubri

I-7 Dieser Gecko kommt ursprünglich aus Südost-Asien.

❖ Bewohnte Gebiete auf San Cristóbal und Santa Cruz.

4 Galápagos-Blattfingergecko

E-7 Eine endemische Art mit sehr unterschiedlicher Färbung.

❖ Santa Cruz, Daphne Major, Pinzón, Santiago, Isabela, und Fernandina.

5 Phyllodactlyus bauri

E-7.

❖ Española und Floreana.

Nicht gezeigt sind die endemischen Geckoarten auf Santa Fé und Wolf, genauso wie zwei weitere Arten auf San Cristóbal.

1 *Gonatodes caudiscutatus*

2 *Phyllodactylus reissi*

4 *Phyllodactylus galapagoensis*

3 *Lepidodactylus lugrubris*

5 *Phyllodactylus bauri*

1 Iguana Terrestre Rosada

E-1 Esta iguana fue estudiada por primera vez en el año 2000, por unos científicos italianos, La población parece ser muy pequeña.

❖ Sólo en zonas poco visitadas del volcán Wolf, en la isla Isabela.

2 Iguana Terrestre

E-3 Los machos son mucho más grandes que las hembras y durante la época de cría guardan celosamente su territorio.

❖ Plaza Sur, Santa Cruz, Seymour Norte.

3 Iguana Terrestre de Santa Fé

E-3 Parecida a la otra iguana terrestre pero de color más pálido.

❖ Sólo en Santa Fé.

4 Iguana Marina

E-3 El único lagarto marino del mundo. Hay siete subespecies con una variedad de tamaños y colores. Se alimenta de algas marinas. Aquí se muestra una iguana gris oscura, típica de Santa Cruz (4a) y un macho colorido, (4b) en Española.

❖ Muy extendida en las costas rocosas.

1 Pink Land Iguana

E-1 First studied by Italian scientists in 2000. The population seems very small.

❖ Only in a rarely visited area of Volcan Wolf, on Isla Isabela.

2 Galápagos Land Iguana

E-3 Males are much larger than the females, and are very territorial in the breeding season.

❖ Plaza Sur, Santa Cruz, Seymour Norte.

3 Santa Fé Land Iguana

E-3 Similar to the other land iguana, but paler in colour.

❖ Only on Santa Fé.

4 Marine Iguana

E-3 The only marine lizard in the world. Seven subspecies, with a variety of sizes and colours. Feeds on marine algae. Shown here are a typical dark grey iguana from Santa Cruz (4a) and a colourful male (4b) from Española.

❖ Widespread on rocky shores.

1 Rosafarbener Landleguan

E-1 Wurde zum ersten Mal 2000 von italienischen Wissenschaftlern untersucht. Die Population scheint sehr klein zu sein.

❖ Nur in einem selten besuchten Gebiet auf dem Vulkan Wolf der Insel Isabela.

2 Landleguan (Drusenkopf)

E-3 Die Männchen sind sehr viel größer als die Weibchen und während der Fortpflanzungszeit sehr territorial.

❖ Plaza Sur, Santa Cruz, Seymour Norte.

3 Santa Fé-Landleguan (Santa Fé-Drusenkopf)

E-3 Dem anderen Landleguan ähnlich aber heller in der Färbung.

❖ Nur auf Santa Fé.

4 Meerechse

E-3 Weltweit die einzige Meerechse. Es gibt sieben Unterarten, die sich in der Größe und der Färbung unterscheiden. Ernährt sich von Meeresalgen. Hier gezeigt ist eine typische dunkelgraue Echse von Santa Cruz (4a) und ein farbenfrohes Männchen (4b) von Española.

❖ Weit verbreitet an felsigen Küsten.

1 *Conolophus marthae*

2 *Conolophus subcristatus*

3 *Conolophus pallidus*

4a

4b

4 *Amblyrhynchus cristatus*

PLANTAS DE ZONAS COSTERAS

COASTAL PLANTS

KÜSTENPFLANZEN

1 Mangle Rojo

N-8 El más común de los mangles de Las Galápagos tiene raíces aéreas, hojas brillantes y unas inconfundibles semillas alargadas (1a). Las ramas más jóvenes son de color rojizo.

❖ Orillas abrigadas y playas, formando a menudo matorrales.

2 Mangle Blanco

N-7 Sus hojas son pálidas y puntuadas en el reverso; algunas de sus raíces son aéreas y sobresalen por encima de la superficie del agua.

❖ Alrededor de los lagos, algunos de los cuales son salobres, en la zona costera.

3 Mangle Botón

N-6 Más pequeño que los otros mangles, con frutos planos y hojas pequeñas y coriáceas.

❖ La zona costera, especialmente en Puerto Ayora, Santa Cruz y Puerto Villamil en Isabela.

4 Mangle Negro

N-8 El mangle más grande de Las Galápagos alcanza los 25 metros. Las hojas son oscuras por encima y más pálidas por debajo. Sus frutos flotan y se dispersan en el océano.

❖ Zonas costeras, cerca de las playas arenosas y los lagos salobres.

1 Red Mangrove

N-8 Most common of the mangroves in Galapagos. It has prop roots, waxy leaves, and distinctive seedlings (1a). The young branches are reddish in colour.

❖ Sheltered shores and beaches, often forms thickets.

2 White mangrove

N-7 Pale-coloured leaves are spotted above and below. The tree often produces roots above the ground.

❖ Around lagoons, some of them brackish, in the Coastal zone.

3 Button Mangrove

N-6 Smaller than the other mangroves, with flattened fruit and small leathery leaves.

❖ The Coastal zone, especially at Puerto Ayora, Santa Cruz, and Puerto Villamil, Isabela.

4 Black Mangrove

N-8 The largest mangrove in Galapagos, reaching 80 feet (25 metres). Leaves dark above and paler below. Its fruits float and are dispersed in the ocean.

❖ The Coastal zone, near sandy beaches and brackish lagoons.

1 Rote Mangrove

N-8 Die häufigste Mangrovenart auf Galápagos. Sie hat Stützwurzeln, wachsartige Blätter und charakteristische Sämlinge (1a). Die jungen Zweige sind rötlich gefärbt.

❖ Geschützte Ufer und Strände, können Dickicht ausbilden.

2 Weiße Mangrove

N-7 Blassgrüne Blätter mit Punkten an der Blattunterseite, auch außerhalb des Wassers wurzelnd.

❖ Um Lagunen herum, auch in Brackwasser-Lagunen, in der Küstenzone.

3 Knopfmangrove

N-6 Kleiner als die anderen Mangroven, mit abgeflachten Früchten und kleinen, lederartigen Blättern.

❖ In der Küstenzone, besonders in Puerto Ayora, Santa Cruz, und Puerto Villamil, Isabela.

4 Schwarze Mangrove

N-8 Die kleinste Mangrove auf Galápagos, erreicht eine Höhe von 25 m. Blätter sind auf der Oberseite dunkel und auf der Unterseite hell. Die Früchte schwimmen und werden vom Meer verbreitet.

❖ In der Küstenzone, in der Nähe von sandigen Stränden und Brackwasser-Lagunen.

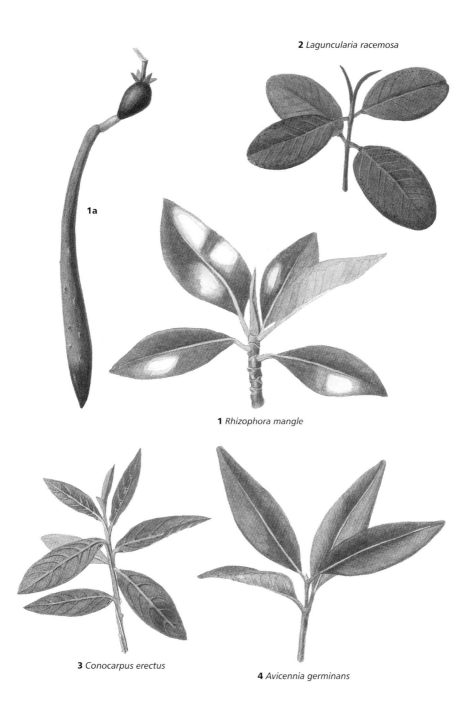

2 *Laguncularia racemosa*

1a

1 *Rhizophora mangle*

3 *Conocarpus erectus*

4 *Avicennia germinans*

1 Uva de Playa

N-5 Los frutos maduros de esta planta parecen uvas.

❖ En o cerca de la playas.

2 Monte Salado

N-8 Un arbusto de baja altura que tolera la sal y forma densos matorrales.

❖ Zona costera.

3 Satsola

N-6 Otro arbusto costero que forma densos matorrales. Sus flores son diminutas.

❖ Zona costera.

4 Sesuvium

E-6 Una hierba baja de hojas carnosas. Durante la estación seca adquiere un color rojo brillante (4a) y se vuelve verde después de las lluvias.

❖ Zonas rocosas, especialmente en Plaza Sur.

5 Nolana

E-5 Un arbusto con hojas en forma bastoncillo y flores en forma de campana.

❖ Cerca de la orilla.

6 Portulaca

E-5 Tras la lluvia a esta hierba le crecen las hojas y unas flores amarillas.

❖ En las rocas de lava cerca de la orilla.

7 Ipomoea

N-7 Una enredadera que llega a alcanzar los 10 metros de longitud, con grandes flores de color violeta.

❖ Muy extendida en las playas arenosas.

8 Polygala

E-6 Existen diversas variedades de esta planta. Esta es una hierba erguida con pequeñas flores blancas que alcanza los 60 cm.

❖ Zonas áridas cerca de la costa.

1 Sea Grape

N-5 The mature fruits do look like grapes.

❖ On or near beaches.

2 Saltbush

N-8 Low-growing and salt-tolerant shrub forming dense thickets.

❖ Coastal zone.

3 Saltwort

N-6 Another coastal shrub that forms dense thickets. Its flowers are tiny.

❖ Coastal zone.

4 Galápagos Carpetweed

E-6 Low-lying herb with fleshy leaves. Bright red in dry season (4a), green after rain.

❖ Rocky areas, especially South Plaza.

5 Galápagos Clubleaf

E-5 A shrub with club-shaped leaves and bell-shaped flowers.

❖ Close to shore.

6 Galápagos Purslane

E-5 A herb that grows leaves and yellow flowers after rain.

❖ Lava rocks close to the shore.

7 Beach Morning Glory

N-7 A vine with stems up to 10 metres long; large purple flowers.

❖ Widespread on sandy beaches.

8 St. George's Milkwort

E-6 There are several varieties of this plant. The one shown is an erect herb up to 60 cm with small white flowers.

❖ Arid areas near the coast.

1 Scaevola

N-5 Die reifen Früchte sehen wie Weintrauben aus.

❖ An oder in der Nähe von Stränden.

2 Salzbusch

N-8 Niedrig wachsender, salztoleranter Strauch, der ein Dickicht ausbildet.

❖ Küstengebiet.

3 Salzkraut

N-6 Ein anderer Küstenstrauch, der ein Dickicht ausbildet. Seine Blüten sind winzig.

❖ Küstenzone.

4 Galápagos-Sesuvie

E-6 Niedrig wachsendes Kraut mit fleischigen Blättern. Leuchtend rot in der Trockenzeit (4a), grün nach der Regenzeit.

❖ Steinige Gebiete, besonders South Plaza.

5 Galápagos-Nolana

E-5 Ein Strauch mit keulenförmigen Blättern und glockenförmigen Blüten.

❖ In Küstennähe.

6 Galápagos-Portulak

E-5 Ein Kraut, das nach Regen Blätter und gelbe Blüten austreibt.

❖ Lavasteine in Küstennähe.

7 Strandwinde

N-7 Eine Winde, die lange (bis zu 10 m) Ausläufer bildet, mit violetten Blüten.

❖ Weit verbreitet an sandigen Stränden.

8 Galápagos-Polygala

E-6 Es gibt mehrere Varietäten dieser Pflanze. Hier gezeigt ist die St. Georgs Polygala (Kreuzblume).

❖ Trockenzonen in Küstennähe.

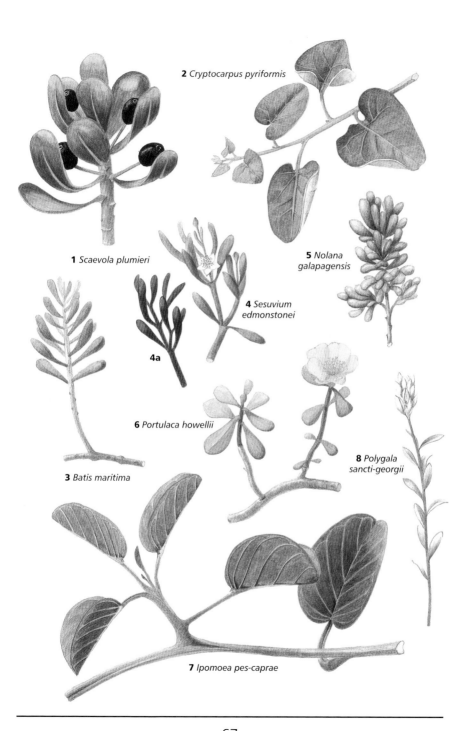

2 *Cryptocarpus pyriformis*

1 *Scaevola plumieri*

5 *Nolana galapagensis*

4 *Sesuvium edmonstonei*

4a

6 *Portulaca howellii*

8 *Polygala sancti-georgii*

3 *Batis maritima*

7 *Ipomoea pes-caprae*

PLANTAS DE ZONAS ÁRIDAS

ARID ZONE PLANTS

PFLANZEN DER TROCKENGEBIETE

1 Matazarno

N-8 La madera de este árbol es muy dura y se utiliza para la construcción de barcos y edificios.

❖ Tierras altas y bajas.

2 Palo Santo

N-9 Es pariente del incienso y se quema como tal en las iglesias; también se utiliza como repelente de mosquitos.

❖ Muy extendido.

3 Arrayancillo

N-8 Un árbol de poca altura con hojas brillantes y frutos rojos.

❖ Zonas áridas y costeras.

4 Tuna

E-7 Existen siete especies diferentes y muchas variedades de este cáctus que es un ejemplo de radiación adaptativa. Este ejemplar se encuentra en Santa Cruz.

❖ Zonas bajas y áridas.

5 Cacto Candelabro

E-3 Esta especie tiene tres variedades que llegan a alcanzar los siete metros.

❖ Muy extendido, especialmente en Santa Cruz, cerca de la Estación Científica Charles Darwin y en Floreana, en Punta Cormorán.

6 Cacto de Lava

E-5 Una planta pionera que crece sólo en la lava desnuda.

❖ Algunas de las islas grandes, especialmente Fernandina, Santiago y Genovesa.

1 Piscidia

N-8 The wood of this tree is very hard and is used in boat-building and construction.

❖ Lowlands and highlands.

2 Holy Stick

N-9 It is related to frankincense and is burned in churches as incense, and is also used as a mosquito repellent.

❖ Widespread.

3 Leatherleaf

N-8 A fairly low-growing tree with waxy leaves and red fruits.

❖ Arid and Coastal Zones.

4 Prickly Pear Cactus

E-7 There are six different species and many varieties of this cactus which is an example of adaptive radiation. The one shown is on Santa Cruz.

❖ Arid lowlands.

5 Candelabra Cactus

E-5 This species has three varieties, up to 7 m.

❖ Widespread, especially Santa Cruz, near CDRS and Floreana at Punta Cormoran.

6 Lava Cactus

E-5 A pioneer plant found only on bare lava.

❖ Several larger islands, especially Fernandina, Santiago, and Genovesa.

1 Matazarno

N-8 Das Holz dieses Baumes ist extrem hart und wird daher im Boots-und Hausbau verwendet.

❖ Flach-und Hochlad.

2 Balsambaum

N-9 Ist verwandt mit dem Weihrauchbaum und sein Harz wird in Kirchen verbrannt. Es wird auch als Mückenschutz verwendet.

❖ Weit verbreitet.

3 Maytenus

N-8 Ein recht kleinwüchsiger Baum mit wachsartigen Blättern und roten Früchten.

❖ Trocken-und Küstenzone.

4 Galápagos-Feigenkaktus

E-7 Es gibt sechs verschiedenen Arten und viele Varietäten dieses Kaktus, was ein Beispiel für eine adaptive Radiation ist. Der gezeigte Kaktus ist von Santa Cruz.

❖ Trockenes Flachland.

5 Galápagos-Säulenkaktus

E-3 Diese Art teilt sich in drei Varietäten auf, die gezeigte ist von Santa Cruz.

❖ Alle größeren Inseln, besonders nahe der Darwin Station auf Santa Cruz und am Punta Cormoran auf Floreana.

6 Galápagos-Lavakaktus

E-5 Eine Pionierpflanze, die sich auf nackter Lava ansiedelt.

❖ Verschiedene größere Inseln, besonders Fernandina, Santiago und Genovesa.

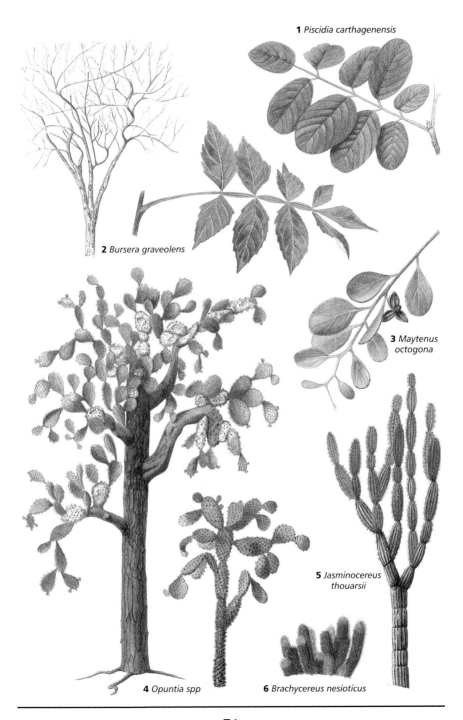

1 *Piscidia carthagenensis*

2 *Bursera graveolens*

3 *Maytenus octogona*

4 *Opuntia spp*

5 *Jasminocereus thouarsii*

6 *Brachycereus nesioticus*

1 Acacia

N/E-7 Existen varias especies de aspecto similar, una de ellas es endémica y con grandes espinas.

❖ En la mayoría de las islas más grandes.

2 Palo Verde

N-7 Árbol de ramas desplegadas, con hojas largas y caídas, que a su vez pueden estar formadas por muchos pares de hojitas.

❖ En la mayoría de las islas más grandes.

3 Chala

E-7 Un árbol o arbusto con una savia que puede dejar manchas permanentes de color marrón en la ropa.

❖ Muy extendido.

4 Muyuyo

N-7 Cuando se exprime, su fruto es extremadamente pegajoso (¡muy útil para cerrar sobres!).

❖ En la mayoría de las islas más grandes, incluyendo Post Office Bay en Floreana.

5 Flamboyán

I-5 Árbol originario de Madagascar con unas llamativas flores rojas.

❖ Se encuentra en Santa Cruz y en otras islas habitadas.

6 Manzanillo

N-6 La savia y los frutos de este árbol que parecen manzanas, son muy venenosos y no deben nunca comerse ni tocarse.

❖ En las islas habitadas y también en la playa Espumilla Beach en Santiago.

1 Acacia

N/E-7 There are several similar-looking species, with large thorns, one of them endemic.

❖ Most of the larger islands.

2 Jerusalem Thorn

N-7 A tree with spreading branches that have long, drooping leaves. These bear many pairs of leaflets.

❖ Most of the larger islands.

3 Galápagos Croton

E-7 A shrub or tree with sap that can leave permanent brown stains on clothing.

❖ Widespread.

4 Yellow Cordia

N-7 When crushed, its fruit becomes extremely sticky (useful for sealing envelopes!).

❖ Most of the larger islands, including Floreana, at Post Office Bay.

5 Flamboyant

I-5 Originally from Madagascar, its bright red flowers are very striking.

❖ Found on Santa Cruz and other inhabited islands.

6 Poison Apple

N-6 This tall tree has sap and fruits that look like apples. These are very poisonous, and should never be touched or eaten.

❖ The main islands, especially Santa Cruz at Puerto Ayora, and Santiago at Espumilla Beach.

1 Akazie

N/E-7 Es gibt mehrere ähnliche Arten, mit langen Dornen, eine davon endemisch.

❖ Auf den meisten größeren Inseln.

2 Parkinsonie

N-7 Ein Baum mit ausladenden Zweigen, die lange, hängende Blätter haben. Diese sind mit vielen Fiederpaarblättchen besetzt.

❖ Auf den meisten größeren Inseln.

3 Galápagos-Croton

E-7 Ein Strauch oder Baum mit Milchsaft, der permanente Flecken auf der Kleidung hinterlässt.

❖ Weit verbreitet.

4 Gelbe Cordie

N-7 Die gequetschten Früchte sind ausgesprochen klebrig (können zum Zukleben von Briefen verwendet werden!).

❖ Auf den meisten größeren Inseln, auch Floreana, an der Post Office Bay.

5 Flammenbaum (Flamboyant)

I-5 Ursprünglich von Madagaskar, seine leuchtend roten Blüten sind sehr auffällig.

❖ Auf Santa Cruz und anderen bewohnten Inseln.

6 Mancinellenbaum

N-6 Dieser große Baum hat Milchsaft und Früchte, die wie Äpfeln aussehen. Diese sind sehr giftig und sollten niemals berührt oder gegessen werden.

❖ Auf den Hauptinseln, besonders Santa Cruz in Puerto Ayora und Santiago, am Espumilla-Strand.

1 *Acacia spp*

2 *Parkinsonia aculeata*

3 *Croton scouleri*

4 *Cordia lutea*

5 *Delonix regia*

6 *Hippomane mancinella*

73

1 Darwiniothamnus

E-4 Crece en la mayoría de los habitats, desde las tierras bajas a las altas.

❖ En las islas más grandes del centro y del oeste.

2 Algodón de Galápagos

E-7 Arbusto de gran altura, bastante extendido. Las aves pequeñas utilizan las hilachas para forrar sus nidos.

❖ En las islas más grandes. Florece especialmente tras las lluvias copiosas.

3 Espino

E-8 Las espinas de este arbusto alcanzan los 6 cm de longitud. Muy extendido cerca las orillas de muchas islas.

❖ Presente en muchas zonas de interés para los visitantes.

4 Tomatillo de Galápagos

E-6 Hay dos especies endémicas de tomates y dos introducidas. Los frutos de las primeras son de color naranja o amarillo y los de las segundas rojo brillante.

❖ En las islas habitadas.

5 Flor de la pasión

N-8 Planta trepadora, originaria de América tropical, que crece en todos los hábitats. .

❖ En Santa Cruz, en Puerto Ayora y en Isabela y Floreana.

6 Waltheria

N-8 Un pequeño arbusto muy extendido en las zonas bajas y áridas; también crece en Perú.

❖ En Santa Cruz.

7 Tournefortia

E-7 Arbusto con ramas blancas y peludas que alcanza los cuatro metros de altura.

❖ En Santa Cruz, en la carretera al aeropuerto.

1 Thin-leafed Darwin's Shrub

E-4 Found in most habitats, from lowlands to highlands.

❖ Most of the larger islands.

2 Galápagos Cotton

E-7 This tall shrub is not cultivated, but small birds use the lint to line their nests.

❖ In the larger islands.

3 Thorn Shrub

E-8 The sharp thorns on this bush are up to 6 cm long. It is widespread near the shore of many islands.

❖ It is present at many visitor sites.

4 Galápagos Tomato

E-6 There are two endemic species and two introduced species of tomato in the islands. The former have orange or yellow fruit, while the others' fruits are bright red.

❖ Widespread on the inhabited islands.

5 Passion Flower

N-7 Originally from tropical America, this climbing vine is found in all habitats.

❖ In Santa Cruz at Puerto Ayora, and on Isabela and Floreana.

6 Waltheria

N-8 A small shrub in the arid lowlands.

❖ Widespread.

7 White-haired Tournefortia

E-7 A shrub with white hairy branches up to 4 m tall.

❖ Santa Cruz, on the airport road.

1 Darwiniothamnus

E-4 In verschiedenen Habitaten anzutreffen, vom Tief- zum Hochland.

❖ Auf den meisten größeren Inseln.

2 Galápagos-Baumwolle

E-7 Dieser große Strauch wird nicht kultiviert, aber kleine Vögel benutzen die Fasern, um ihre Nester damit auszulegen.

❖ Auf den größeren Inseln.

3 Scutia

E-8 Die spitzen Dornen dieses Strauches werden bis zu 6 cm lang. Er ist in Küstennähe verschiedener Inseln weit verbreitet.

❖ Kommt an den meisten Touristenorten vor.

4 Galápagos-Tomate

E-6 Es gibt zwei endemische und zwei eingeführte Tomatenarten auf den Inseln. Erstere haben orangefarbene oder gelbe Früchte, während die Früchte der letzteren leuchtend rot sind.

❖ Weit verbreitet auf den bewohnten Inseln.

5 Passionsblume

N-7 Diese Kletterpflanze ist in allen Habitaten anzutreffen.

❖ Auf Santa Cruz, in Puerto Ayora, und auf Isabela und Floreana.

6 Waltheria

N-8 Ein kleiner Strauch des trockenem Tieflands.

❖ Weit verbreitet.

7 Tournefortia pubescens

E-7 Ein Strauch mit behaarten Zweigen, der bis zu 4 m hoch wird.

❖ Santa Cruz, an der Flughafenstraße

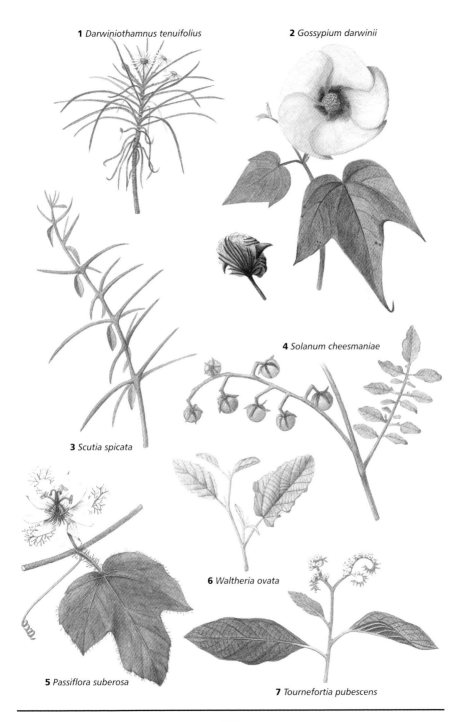

1 *Darwiniothamnus tenuifolius*

2 *Gossypium darwinii*

4 *Solanum cheesmaniae*

3 *Scutia spicata*

6 *Waltheria ovata*

5 *Passiflora suberosa*

7 *Tournefortia pubescens*

1 Tiquilia

E-3 Una de las tres especies, muy parecidas entre si, de plantas pioneras de baja altura. Crece con fuerza en zonas de arena y ceniza volcánica.

❖ En Bartolomé y en Sullivan Bay en Santiago.

2 Cyperus

E-7 Existen 18 especies de juncos en Las Galápagos, que a menudo se confunden con hierbas.

❖ Desde la costa hasta las tierras altas.

3 Monte Colorado

E-7 Existen siete subespecies de este arbusto en Las Galápagos. Sus ramas se vuelven marrones cuando no llueve.

❖ Tierras bajas y áridas.

4 Monte Colorado

E-7 Esta especie tiene las flores blancas y espinosas.

❖ Tierras bajas y áridas.

5 Amargo

E-6 Los frutos de este arbusto son de un rojo brillante y muy amargos.

❖ Zonas de lava rocosa en las islas más grandes.

6 Chamaesyce

E-6 Un pequeño arbusto con una savia blanca y lechosa y flores diminutas.

❖ En Genovesa y en Bartolomé.

7 Lecocarpus

E-3 Este arbusto crece sólo en una isla.

❖ En Punta Cormoran, en Floreana.

8 Lantana de Galápagos

E-8 A menudo crece en densos matorrales y sus flores son blancas con el centro amarillo.

❖ Muy extendida.

---

1 Tiquilia

E-3 One of three very similar species of low-growing pioneer plants. Thrives in areas of sand and volcanic ash.

❖ Bartolomé and Santiago at Sullivan Bay.

2 Anderson's Sedge

E-7 There are 18 species of sedge in Galápagos, which are often confused with grasses.

❖ From the coast to the highlands.

3 Thread-leafed Chaff Flower

E-7 There are 7 subspecies of this shrub in Galápagos. Their branches turn brown in the dry season.

❖ Arid lowlands.

4 Spiny-headed Chaff Flower

N-7 This species has white spiny flowers.

❖ Arid lowlands.

5 Bitterbush

E-6 The bright red fruits of this shrub are extremely bitter.

❖ Rocky lava areas on the larger islands.

6 Chamaesyce

E-6 A small shrub with a milky-white sap and tiny flowers.

❖ Widespread.

7 Wing-fruited Lecocarpus

E-3 This shrub is found on only one island.

❖ Punta Cormorán on Floreana.

8 Galápagos Lantana

E-8 Often grows in dense thickets; its white flowers have yellow centres.

❖ Widespread.

---

1 Tiquilia

E-3 Eine von drei sehr ähnlichen, flach wachsenden Pionierpflanzen. Wächst gut in Gebieten mit Sand und vulkanischer Asche.

❖ Bartolomé und Santiago, am Sullivan-Strand.

2 Segge

E-7 Es gibt 18 Seggenarten auf Galápagos, die oft mit Gräsern verwechselt werden.

❖ Von der Küste bis zum Hochland.

3 Alternanthera

E-7 Es gibt 7 Unterarten dieses Strauches auf Galápagos. Ihre Zweige färben sich während der Trockenzeit braun.

❖ Trockenes Tiefland.

4 Alternanthera

N-7 Diese Art hat weiße, stachelige Blüten.

❖ Trockenes Tiefland.

5 Galápagos-Castela

E-6 Die leuchtend roten Früchte dieses Strauches sind extrem bitter.

❖ Felsige Lavagebiete der größeren Inseln.

6 Chamaesyce

E-6 Ein kleiner Strauch mit weißem Milchsaft und winzigen Blüten.

❖ Weit verbreitet.

7 Floreana-Lecocarpus

E-3 Diesen Strauch gibt es nur auf einer einzigen Insel.

❖ Punta Cormorán, auf Floreana.

8 Galápagos-Wandelröschen

E-8 Wächst häufig im Dickicht, seine weißen Blüten sind in der Mitte gelb.

❖ Weit verbreitet.

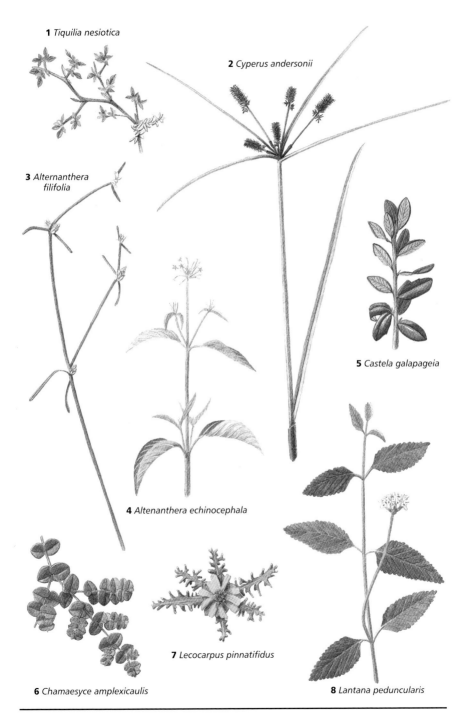

1 *Tiquilia nesiotica*

2 *Cyperus andersonii*

3 *Alternanthera filifolia*

4 *Altenanthera echinocephala*

5 *Castela galapageia*

6 *Chamaesyce amplexicaulis*

7 *Lecocarpus pinnatifidus*

8 *Lantana peduncularis*

PLANTAS DE ZONAS HÚMEDAS

HUMID ZONE PLANTS

PFLANZEN IN FEUCHTGEBIETEN

1 Huaycundu

E-7 Esta planta de tallos largos es miembro de la familia de las piñas. Es una epifita de hoja perenne que crece principalmente en las zonas húmedas.

❖ En las tierras altas de Santa Cruz.

2 Lechoso

E-3 Este árbol crece hasta alcanzar los 15 metros, formando bosques en las tierras altas de varias islas. Es de la misma familia que el diente de león, el girasol y la margarita.

❖ En Santa Cruz, cerca de Los Gemelos.

3 Muérdago de Galápagos

E-6 Un arbusto parásito que carece de raíces y que realiza su propia fotosíntesis.

❖ Raro, pero muy extendido en las islas grandes.

4 Guayabillo

E-7 Árbol o arbusto que llega a alcanzar los ocho metros de altura. Sus frutos, al contrario que los de la guava, introducida en las islas, no tienen mucho sabor.

❖ En Santa Cruz y en Volcán Sierra Negra, en Isabela.

5 Orquídea de Galápagos

E-7 Una epifita de hoja perenne que crece en los árboles y a menudo cuelga hacia abajo. Está muy extendida en las tierras altas.

❖ En Los Gemelos, en Santa Cruz.

6 Café

I-9 La conocida planta del café, originaria de África, que fue introducida y cultivada en las islas y que ha escapado a las zonas boscosas de las islas habitadas.

❖ Tierras altas de Santa Cruz y en San Cristobal y Floreana.

1 Galápagos Bromeliad

E-7 This long-stalked member of the pineapple family is a perennial epiphyte found mainly in the humid areas.

❖ Highlands of Santa Cruz.

2 Tree Scalesia

E-3 This tree grows to 15 m and forms forests in the highlands of several islands. It is related to dandelions, sunflowers, and daisies.

❖ Santa Cruz near Los Gemelos.

3 Galápagos Mistletoe

E-6 This shrub is a hemiparasite and lacks a root system, so it does its own photosynthesis.

❖ Uncommon but widespread on most of the larger islands.

4 Galápagos Guava

E-7 Shrub or tree up to 8 m, with greyish bark. Unlike the introduced guava, its fruits are not very tasty.

❖ The larger islands, especially Santa, Cruz and Isabela at Volcán Sierra Negra.

5 Galápagos Orchid

E-7 An epiphytic perennial growing on trees, and often hanging downwards. It is locally common in highland areas.

❖ Santa Cruz at Los Gemelos.

6 Coffee

I-9 This is the familiar coffee, originally from Africa, which has been introduced in the highlands. Coffee cultivation is steadily increasing in the agricultural areas.

❖ Highlands of Santa Cruz, San Cristóbal, and Floreana.

1 Galápagos-Bromelie

E-7 Dieser langgestielte Vertreter der Bromeliengewächse ist ein mehrjähriger Epiphyt, der in feuchten Gebieten vorkommt.

❖ Hochland von Santa Cruz.

2 Sonnenblumenbaum

E-3 Dieser Baum erreicht eine Höhe von bis zu 15 m und bildet auf verschiedenen Inseln dichte Bestände aus. Er ist verwandt mit Löwenzahn, Sonnenblume und Gänseblümchen.

❖ Santa Cruz, in der Nähe von Los Gemelos.

3 Galápagos-Mistel

E-6 Dieser Strauch ist ein Halbschmarotzer, da er zwar keine Wurzeln besitzt, aber seine eigene Photosythese betreibt.

❖ Nicht häufig aber weit verbreitet auf den meißten größeren Inseln.

4 Galápagos-Guave

E-7 Ein bis zu 8 m grosser Strauch oder Baum, mit grauer Borke. Anders als bei der eingeführten Guave, sind die Früchte nicht sehr schmackhaft.

❖ Auf den größeren Inseln, besonders Santa Cruz und Volcán Sierra Negra auf Isabela.

5 Galápagos-Orchidee

E-7 Eine mehrjährige Orchidee, die auf Bäumen und oftmals nach unten gerichtet wächst. Sie kommt gelegentlich gehäuft im Hochland vor.

❖ Santa Cruz, bei Los Gemelos.

6 Kaffee

I-9 Dieses ist der gewöhnliche Kaffee, der ursprünglich aus Afrika kommt und im Hochland eingeführt wurde. Der Kaffeeanbau in den Landwirtschaftszonen von Galápagos nimmt kontinuierlich zu.

❖ Hochland von Santa Cruz, San Cristóbal und Floreana.

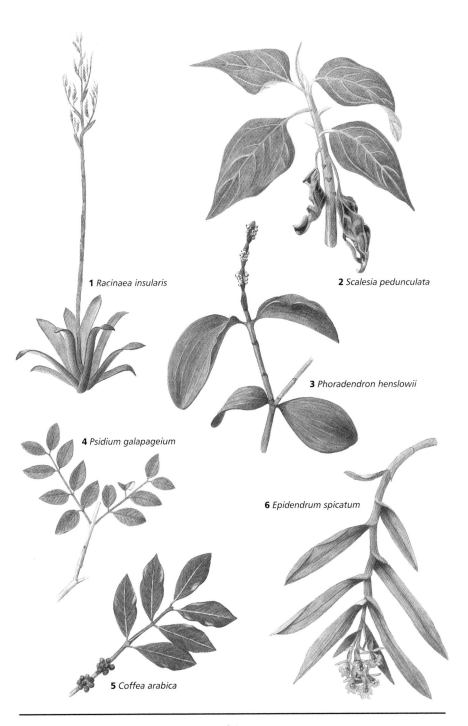

1 *Racinaea insularis*

2 *Scalesia pedunculata*

3 *Phoradendron henslowii*

4 *Psidium galapageium*

6 *Epidendrum spicatum*

5 *Coffea arabica*

1 Cacaotillo

E-3 Un arbusto que puede llegar a alcanzar los cinco metros de altura y que se encuentra amenazado por especies introducidas como las mora y la cascarilla.

❖ En las tierras altas de Santa Cruz y de San Cristóbal.

2 Cascarilla

I-7 Este árbol fue introducido en los años cuarenta por el valor comercial de la quinina que se extrae de su corteza. Ahora constituye una grave amenaza para las plantas nativas.

❖ En las tierras altas de Santa Cruz.

3 Mora

I-9 Introducida y cultivada por sus frutos, constituye ahora un serio peligro par las especies nativas.

❖ En las tierras altas de las islas más importantes.

4 Lycopodiella

N-6 Una de las ocho especies de licopodio que crecen en las Galápagos y que son parientes de los helechos.

❖ Principalmente en las tierras altas de varias islas.

5 Helecho arbóreo

E-7 Un helecho arbóreo que alcanza los seis metros de altura.

❖ En las tierras altas de Santa Cruz, en Los Gemelos y Media Luna.

6 Chontillo

N-9 Un gran helecho ramificado, muy parecido a las especies de helechos de otros países.

❖ En las tierras altas de Santa Cruz, Isabela y San Cristóbal.

1 Galápagos Miconia

E-3 A shrub up to 5 m tall that is threatened by introduced species, such as hill raspberry and quinine trees.

❖ Highlands of Santa Cruz and San Cristóbal.

2 Quinine Tree

I-7 This tree was introduced in the 1940s as a cash crop valued for the quinine in its bark. It is now a serious threat to the native plants.

❖ Highlands of Santa Cruz.

3 Hill Raspberry

I-9 Introduced and cultivated for its fruits but now a serious pest species.

❖ Highlands of all the major islands.

4 Galápagos Club Moss

N-6 One of 8 species of Clubmoss in Galápagos. They are related to ferns.

❖ Mainly in highlands of several islands.

5 Galápagos Tree Fern

E-7 A large fern growing to 6 m.

❖ Highlands of Santa Cruz at Los Gemelos and Media Luna,.

6 Bracken

N-9 A large branching fern very similar to bracken species in other countries,.

❖ Highlands of Santa Cruz, Isabela, and San Cristóbal.

1 Galápagos-Miconia

E-3 Dieser bis zu 5 m hohe Strauch ist von eingeführten Pflanzenarten, wie Brombeere und dem Chinarindenbaum, gefährdet.

❖ Hochland von Santa Cruz und San Cristóbal.

2 Chinarindenbaum

I-7 Dieser Baum wurde in den 40-er Jahren wegen seines Chiningehaltes in der Rinde als landwirtschaftliche Nutzpflanze eingeführt. Er stellt nun eine ernsthafte Bedrohung für die einheimischen Pflanzen dar.

❖ Hochland von Santa Cruz.

3 Brombeere

I-9 Wurde aufgrund der Früchte eingeführt und stellt nun eine ernsthafte Plage dar.

❖ Hochland der größeren Inseln.

4 Bärlapp

N-6 Eine von 8 Bärlapparten auf Galápagos. Sie sind mit den Farnen verwandt.

❖ Hauptsächlich im Hochland verschiedener Inseln.

5 Galápagos-Baumfarn

E-7 Ein großer, bis zu 6 m hoher Farn.

❖ Hochland von Santa Cruz, bei Los Gemelos und Media Luna.

6 Adlerfarn

N-9 Großer, verzweigter Farn, ähnlich den Adlerfarnen in anderen Ländern.

❖ Hochland von Santa Cruz, Isabela und San Cristóbal.

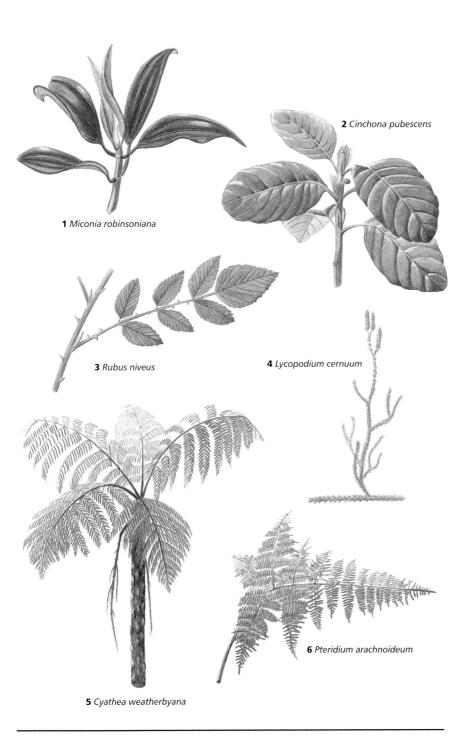

1 *Miconia robinsoniana*

2 *Cinchona pubescens*

3 *Rubus niveus*

4 *Lycopodium cernuum*

5 *Cyathea weatherbyana*

6 *Pteridium arachnoideum*

1 Scalesia helleri

E-3 Arbusto que puede alcanzar los dos metros de altura y cuenta con dos subespecies.

❖ Se encuentra sólo en Santa Cruz y en Santa Fe, principalmente en los acantilados costeros.

2 Scalesia villosa

E-3 Un arbusto muy raro que llega a alcanzar los dos metros de altura.

❖ Sólo en Punta Cormorán, en Floreana y en los islotes cercanos.

3 Scalesia atractyloides

E-1 Un árbol pequeño y muy raro que llega a alcanzar los cinco metros de altura.

❖ Sólo en Santiago.

4 Scalesia affinis

E-5 Un arbusto que parece un árbol y que alcanza los tres metros de altura.

❖ En Santa Cruz y sobre todo en la Cala Tagus, en Isabela.

5 Scalesia stewartii

E-3 Un arbusto con aspecto de árbol que alcanza los tres metros de altura.

❖ En Bartolomé y en la Bahía de Sullivan en Santiago.

6 Scalesia crockeri

E-3 Un arbusto pequeño que alcanza los dos metros de altura.

❖ En Baltra y al norte de Santa Cruz.

1 Heller's Scalesia

E-3 Shrub that grows up to 2.5 m and has two sub-species.

❖ Found only on Santa Cruz and Santa Fé, mainly on sea cliffs.

2 Longhaired Scalesia

E-3 Very rare shrub that grows up to 2 m.

❖ Only at Punta Cormorán on Floreana and nearby islets.

3 Scalesia atractyloides

E-1 Extremely rare small tree that grows up to 5 m.

❖ Only on Santiago.

4 Radiate-headed Scalesia

E-5 Tree-like shrub that grows up to 3 m.

❖ Santa Cruz, and especially Tagus Cove on Isabela.

5 Stewart's Scalesia

E-3 Tree-like shrub that grows up to 3 m.

❖ Bartolomé and Sullivan Bay on Santiago.

6 Crocker's Scalesia

E-3 Small shrub that grows up to 2 m.

❖ Baltra and northen Santa Cruz.

1 Scalesia helleri

E-3 Ein bis zu 2.5 m hoher Strauch. Es gibt zwei Unterarten.

❖ Nur auf Santa Cruz und Santa Fé, hauptsächlich an Meeresfelsen.

2 Scalesia villosa

E-3 Sehr seltener Strauch, der bis zu 2 m erreicht.

❖ Nur am Punta Cormorán auf Floreana und auf benachbarten kleineren Inseln.

3 Scalesia atractyloides

E-1 Ein extrem seltener Baum, der bis zu 5 m hoch wird. Es gibt zwei Unterarten.

❖ Nur auf Santiago.

4 Scalesia affinis

E-5 Ein baumartiger, bis zu 3 m hoher Strauch. Es gibt drei Unterarten.

❖ Santa Cruz und besonders Tagus Cove auf Isabela.

5 Scalesia stewartii

E-3 Ein baumartiger, bis zu 3 m hoher Strauch.

❖ Bartolomé und Sullivan Bay auf Santiago.

6 Scalesia crockeri

E-3 Kleiner, bis zu 2 m hoher Strauch.

❖ Baltra und nördliches Santa Cruz.

1 *Scalesia helleri*

2 *Scalesia villosa*

4 *Scalesia affinis*

3 *Scalesia atractyloides*

5 *Scalesia stewartii*

6 *Scalesia crockeri*

1 Blechnum polypodioides

N-9 Un helecho de pequeño o mediano tamaño, con los frondes agrupados en racimos y las esporas agregadas a lo largo de la nervadura de las hojitas individuales.

❖ Muy extendido en las tierras altas de la mayoría de las islas más grandes.

2 Blechnum occidentale

N-8 Parecido al anterior pero más grande. Los brotes nuevos suelen ser de color bronce o violeta.

❖ Muy extendido en las tierras altas de la mayoría de las islas más grandes.

3 Polypodium tridens

E-7 Un helecho que alcanza el metro de altura, con frondes rígidos cubiertos de escamas marrones.

❖ Es común en las tierras altas de la mayoría de las islas grandes, especialmente en Santa Cruz, en Los Gemelos.

4 Thelypteris oligocarpa

N-7 Un helecho de mediano tamaño con muchos frondes en racimos y esporas agrupadas en soros negros y redondos en el envés.

❖ En las tierras altas de las islas más grandes.

5 Nephrolepis pectinata

N-9 Un helecho de mediano tamaño con frondes erectos de color verde grisáceo, pinados y dentados.

❖ Muy extendido en las tierras altas de las islas más grandes.

6 Ctenitis sloanei

N-7 Un helecho grande con frondes anchos y pinados, de color verde claro, finamente divididos en tres partes.

❖ En las islas mas grandes.

1 Narrowleaf Midsorus fern.

N-9 This small to medium sized fern has clustered fronds with its spores aggregated along the lower midrib of the individual leaflets.

❖ Widespread in the highlands of most major islands.

2 Hammock fern

N-8 Similar to the Narrowleaf Midsorus but larger. New growth often purple or bronze.

❖ Widespread in the highlands of most major islands.

3 Polypodium tridens

E-7 Fern up to 1 m height with stiff fronds covered in brown scales.

❖ Locally common in highlands of most major islands, especially on Santa Cruz at Los Gemelos.

4 Maiden fern

N-7 Medium-sized fern with many clustered fronds, spores aggregated in black round sori on the lower surface.

❖ Highlands of most major islands.

5 Toothed sword fern

N-9 Medium-sized fern with greyish-green erect fronts with toothed pinnae.

❖ Widespread in the highlands of most major islands.

6 Florida lace fern

N-7 Large fern with broad, light-green fronds and finely triple divided pinnae.

❖ Highlands of most major islands.

1 Kleiner Rippenfarn

N-9 Dieser kleine bis mittelgroße Farn hat dicht zusammengedrängte Farnwedel.

❖ Weit verbreitet im Hochland der meisten größeren Inseln.

2 Großer Rippenfarn

N-8 Ähnlich dem kleinen Rippenfarn, aber größer. Junge Farnwedel sind oft violett oder bronzefarben.

❖ Weit verbreitet im Hochland der meisten größeren Inseln.

3 Polypodium tridens

E-7 Ein bis zu1 m hoher Farn mit steifen Farnwedeln, die mit braunen Schuppen bedeckt sind.

❖ Örtlich häufig im Hochland der meisten größeren Inseln, vor allem bei Los Gemelos auf Santa Cruz.

4 Sumpffarn

N-7 Mittelgroßer Farn mit vielen, dicht zusammengedrängten Farnwedeln.

❖ Hochland der meißten größeren Inseln.

5 Schwertfarn

N-9 Mittelgroßer Farn mit grau-grünen aufrechten Farnwedeln.

❖ Weit verbreitet im Hochland der meisten größeren Inseln.

6 Wurmfarn

N-7 Großer Farn mit breiten, hellgrünen Farnwedeln und dreigeteilten Fiederblättern.

❖ Hochland der meißten größeren Inseln

2 *Polypodium tridens*

1 *Blechnum polypodioides*

3 *Thelypteris oligocarpa*

4 *Blechnum occidentale*

6 *Ctenitis sloanei*

5 *Nephrolepis pectinata*

87

Generalidades

Descubrimiento

Es posible que las islas Galápagos fueran descubiertas por los chimúes y visitadas por el rey inca Tupac Yupanqui, en el siglo XV, pero no hay elementos claros que lo confirmen. El primer descubrimiento documentado data de 1535, cuando un barco que navegaba hacia Perú, en el que viajaba Fray Tomás de Berlanga, Obispo de Panamá, se desvió de su rumbo y llegó a las Galápagos. Unos cuantos años más tarde, otro grupo de españoles desembarcó accidentalmente en las islas. Los informes de ambos viajes enfatizaban la apariencia severa del paisaje de las Galápagos y la falta de agua dulce, elementos que no ofrecían muchos incentivos para explorar las islas.

La época pirata

Una vez que se supo que había tierra en mitad del Pacífico y que en las islas había agua dulce, las Galápagos pronto se convirtieron en guarida de piratas y bucaneros que atacaban los barcos españoles, cargados de tesoros y asaltaban los puertos coloniales de lo que es ahora Perú y Ecuador. Empezaron a utilizar las islas a finales del siglo XVI y siguieron haciéndolo hasta principios del XVIII, volviendo a ellas para repostar de agua y combustible, reparar los barcos y cazar tortugas para aprovisionarse de carne. La cala Bucaneer Cove, al noroeste de la isla de Santiago, era uno de los fondeaderos más populares. Aunque eran de diversas nacionalidades, la mayoría de los piratas eran ingleses y franceses.

Balleneros y pescadores de focas

En 1793 y 1794, el capitán de la armada británica James Colnett fondeó en las Galápagos durante un viaje para comprobar las reservas de ballenas. La noticia de que había un número enorme de cetáceos provocó una especie de fiebre del oro y los barcos balleneros comenzaron a llegar a las islas, primero desde Inglaterra y después desde los puertos de Europa y América. Los balleneros se hicieron ricos pero la destrucción de las ballenas fue sistemática. Entre los años 1811 y 1844 operaban en el Pacífico al menos 700 balleneros americanos, a quienes pronto se les unieron los pescadores de focas peleteras, cuyas actividades estuvieron a punto de provocar la extinción de este animal. El hecho que hizo posible esta masiva explotación fue el aparentemente ilimitado suministro de carne fresca que procuraban las gigantescas tortugas. Algunos barcos llegaron a cargar hasta 600 de estas tortugas que podían sobrevivir hasta un año sin comida ni agua. En consecuencia, esta carnicería continuó hasta alrededor de 1865, cuando quedaban ya tan pocas ballenas y focas que no merecía la pena seguir pescando. Esto salvó a las tortugas que quedaban, pero no libró de la extinción a las especies que habitaban las islas de Floreana, Rábida y Santa Fé.

Los primeros pobladores

El primer asentamiento se estableció en Floreana cuando Ecuador se anexionó oficialmente las islas en 1832. Las cosas no habían empezado bien y como después comenzaron a llegar prisioneros, la isla pronto se convirtió en una colonia penal. Los posteriores intentos de colonización que tuvieron lugar en Floreana y en Santa Cruz, al sur de Isabela y en San Cristóbal, fracasaron en su mayor parte, o terminaron en un baño de sangre. Una plantación situada en Progreso, en San Cristóbal, tuvo bastante éxito con la cosecha de caña de azúcar, café y otros productos, pero el gerente, Manuel Cobos, trataba tan mal a sus empleados que se rebelaron y lo mataron en 1904. La última colonia penal, en el sur de Isabela, duró desde 1946 a 1959, para terminar con una fuga en masa de la mayoría de los prisioneros.

En busca de una utopía

La historia de la colonización de las Galápagos tiene también sus aspectos pintorescos. En los años veinte y treinta el mundo empezaba a oír hablar de las islas y los románticos artículos de revistas y periódicos incitaron a varios "buscadores de utopías" a poner rumbo a las islas. En 1926 unos noruegos llegaron a Floreana para montar un negocio de enlatado de pescado que no tuvo éxito. Mientras tanto, otros noruegos se establecieron en Santa Cruz y San Cristóbal. Aunque estos asentamientos fracasaron por varias razones, algunos de los colonos se quedaron definitivamente a vivir allí.

Fue entonces cuando en 1929, Friedrich Ritter, un filósofo alemán un poco enajenado, y su compañera Dore Strauch, llegaron a Floreana. En 1932 se les unieron los también alemanes, Heinz y Margret Wittmer y más tarde un trío compuesto por una baronesa austríaca y sus dos amantes. Los tres grupos no se llevaban bien entre ellos y hacia finales de 1934 sólo quedaron los Wittmer, ya que los otros habían muerto o desaparecido en misteriosas circunstancias. Margret Wittmer murió en paz en el 2000 y su hijo montó una empresa, Rolf Wittmer Turismo, que organiza cruceros por las islas.

En contrapartida, una discreta pareja de americanos, Ainslie y Frances Conway, vivieron en Floreana y en Santiago durante un par de años, antes y después de la Segunda Guerra Mundial, y según parece, gozaron de una estancia muy agradable. Entre otros alemanes que llegaron a Santa Cruz y a San Cristóbal en los años de entre guerras, cabe destacar a los cinco hermanos Angermeyer, cuyos descendientes todavía siguen en las islas.

Hoy en día las Galápagos cuentan con una creciente población de ecuatorianos que trabajan en el turismo, la agricultura y la pesca.

Historia Natural

Orígenes geológicos

Las islas Galápagos se formaron gracias a la actividad volcánica y son muy jóvenes, desde el punto de vista geológico, ya que no tienen más de diez millones de años. Se alzan cerca de la unión de tres enormes placas tectónicas que se encuentran en proceso de separación. La placa de Nazca, en donde se asientan las Galápagos se desplaza hacia el sudeste a una media de 7 cm por año. Según la teoría del "punto caliente" la corteza de la Tierra en la región de las Galápagos se mueve sobre un punto caliente estacionario, causando erupciones periódicas que llevaron a la formación de volcanes que a su vez se transformaron en islas volcánicas. Las más antiguas son las que están más alejadas del punto caliente, como Española y San Cristóbal, donde la actividad volcánica ha cesado. La más joven es Fernandina en el oeste, que se encuentra más o menos sobre el punto caliente. Fernandina y su vecina, Isabela, son en la actualidad las zonas de más actividad volcánica del archipiélago.

Corrientes oceánicas

Varias y poderosas corrientes oceánicas influyen en el clima y la ecología de las Galápagos y no sólo causan fenómenos climáticos importantes como El Niño, sino que su temperatura, dirección y posición influyen en el tipo de peces y vida marina que habita las aguas que rodean a las islas. Esto a su vez afecta a muchos animales que dependen del mar para alimentarse, como las iguanas marinas y las aves marinas. La Corriente Ecuatorial del Sur es la más rápida, mientras que la Corriente de Humboldt fluye desde las aguas más frías del sur. El sistema es complejo, con contra-corrientes como la Contra-Corriente Ecuatorial de Cromwell que fluye en direcciones inesperadas, y las aguas superficiales desplazándose de forma diferente a las de las profundidades.

Clima

Teniendo en cuenta que las islas están situadas en los trópicos, su micro clima es anormalmente seco. Hay dos estaciones: una cálida, de diciembre a junio, con chaparrones cortos y abundantes, cielos principalmente azules y altas temperaturas marinas; y otra más fresca y húmeda, de junio a diciembre (sobre todo en las tierras altas), con cielos más nublados. Esta última estación se llama la garúa y se caracteriza por los vientos del sudeste y por el agua más fría que trae la Corriente de Humboldt. La pluviosidad varía considerablemente con la altitud y es más abundante en las regiones altas que en las bajas. Los años de El Niño a veces traen consigo un aumento de las lluvias en todas las islas. Sin embargo, la temperatura del aire no varía drásticamente, a pesar de la diferencia de las estaciones. En marzo puede sobrepasar los 30° C, mientras que en agosto y septiembre la media es de unos 22° C.

El Niño (La Oscilación del Sur)

Normalmente, una corriente de agua fría fluye desde las Galápagos hacia el oeste, pero de cada cinco a siete años, los vientos alisios del sudeste amainan, causando un gran volumen de agua caliente en la superficie, que se alza desplazándose hacia el este, hacia las Galápagos y hacia Sudamérica. Las temperaturas del agua del mar pueden aumentar de forma dramática, causando tormentas y lluvias torrenciales. Como siempre ocurre en época de Navidad, al fenómeno se le bautizó con el nombre del El Niño. El repentino cambio climático provoca cambios en el ecosistema marino, y como consecuencia de esto, la muerte por inanición de las aves marinas y otros animales que dependen del mar para sobrevivir. En la tierra sin embargo, se produce un aumento abundante de la vegetación, lo que beneficia a las aves terrestres, a los reptiles y a los insectos.

Especies endémicas

Como las Galápagos nunca han formado parte de ningún continente, todos sus animales y plantas llegaron hasta ellas gracias a un proceso llamado "dispersión de larga distancia". Esto significa que fueron transportadas por el aire, por el mar (focas y pingüinos llegaron a nado, mientras que las ratas arroceras y los reptiles lo hicieron arrastrados por balsas de vegetación), o con las aves (las semillas en las tripas, o pegadas a las patas o a las plumas). Si el animal o la planta sobrevivió a la travesía desde tierra firme y fue capaz de reproducirse en las Galápagos, sus descendientes tuvieron que adaptarse a su nuevo hábitat y competir con otros organismos que ya se encontraban allí. Muchos organismos de las Galápagos han estado aislados durante cientos o miles de años y han desarrollado formas tan diferentes de sus antepasados que son considerados como nuevas especies, o especies endémicas, lo que significa que no se encuentran en ningún otro lugar. Son este tipo de procesos los que dan a las Galápagos su fama de "laboratorio de evolución."

Charles Darwin

En su breve visita en 1835, el joven Darwin quedó muy impresionado con la diversidad de las especie que encontró en las Galápagos. Parece ser que este hecho fue el que provocó la cadena de reflexiones que florecería en 1850 con su revolucionaria obra El origen de las especies por medio de la selección natural. Ya apuntaba hacia dicha teoría en su libro El viaje del Beagle, cuando escribió sobre las Galápagos: "De ahí que, tanto en el espacio como en el tiempo, parece que nos hayamos acercado en alguna medida a ese gran hecho, a ese misterio entre los misterios, la primera aparición de nuevos seres en esta Tierra."

Fauna y Flora

Aves marinas

Situadas como están a cientos o miles de kilómetros de tierra firme, las islas Galápagos atraen a una amplia gama de aves marinas que llegan hasta ellas para criar. Se ha estimado en tres cuartos de millón el número de aves en las islas, incluyendo proporciones importantes de la población de algunas especies. Existen 19 especies de aves marinas residentes, de las cuales cinco son endémicas, más algunas migratorias y vagabundas que no crían en las islas. Destacan una especie de pingüino y una de albatros, cuyos ancestros llegarían desde regiones meridionales mucho más frías; un cormorán que no puede volar; la única gaviota nocturna del mundo; la gaviota más rara del mundo; la colonia más grande de piqueros de patas rojas; y dos especies de petreles que comparten el nido, pero uno de ellos lo ocupa durante el día y el otro por la noche.

Aves costeras

Este grupo comprende una variedad de garzas y garcetas, una especie de flamenco, una de pato y varias zancudas y aves migratorias. La lista incluye una especie endémica, la gaviota de la lava, y varias subespecies endémicas. Las aves migratorias son principalmente las que crían en Norteamérica y emigran al sur durante el invierno septentrional.

Aves terrestres

El número de aves terrestres de las Galápagos es pequeño y la mayoría son endémicas. Las 25 o 30 especies o subespecies que crían en las islas no se encuentran en ningún otro lugar. El ave de presa más importante es el halcón de Galápagos que cuenta con un interesante método de cría. Varios machos pueden emparejarse con una hembra y a continuación ayudarle a criar a los pequeños. Esta práctica de cría cooperativa se llama poliandria. Entre las otras especies de aves terrestres se encuentran una paloma, dos papamoscas, un cuco, una curruca y un rascón diminuto que apenas se deja ver aunque es común en las tierras altas. Uno de los grupos más interesantes está compuesto de cuatro especies endémicas de ruiseñores de los cuales sólo una especie habita en cada una de las islas donde se encuentran. Y lo más interesante de todo son las 13 especies de aves, parecidas a los gorriones, que reciben el nombre colectivo de pinzones de Darwin. Cada uno de ellos ha desarrollado una forma pico especializada que le sirve para procurarse diferentes tipos de alimentos, como semillas (grandes o pequeñas), insectos, flores, hojas, etc. Dos de ellos, el pinzón carpintero y el ahora muy raro pinzón de pantano, utilizan ramitas como herramientas para extraer comida de los agujeros en los árboles.

Reptiles

Mientras que los mamíferos dominan la fauna terrestre en la mayor parte del mundo, en las islas Galápagos son los reptiles quienes juegan ese papel. Los más conocidos y más impresionantes son las tortugas gigantes que una vez llegaron a alcanzar los 250.000 ejemplares, pero cuyo número ha sido reducido a unas 15.000. De estos reptiles sobreviven once subespecies o razas, cinco de las cuales se encuentran en Isabela y otras cinco en cinco islas diferentes. La última está representada por un único macho, Lonesome George (Jorge el Solitario) que reside ahora en el centro de investigación de Santa Cruz. Hay tres especies de iguanas terrestres y una especie de iguana marina que cría en tierra pero se alimenta de algas marinas. Además hay siete especies endémicas de lagartos de lava y seis especies endémicas de salamanquesas. Finalmente, hay varias especies de pequeñas y delgadas serpientes endémicas, que son bastante comunes y están bastante extendidas, pero que apenas se dejan ver.

Mamíferos

Los únicos mamíferos terrestres, nativos de las Galápagos, son dos tipos de murciélagos y cuatro especies de pequeños roedores. Existen varias especies de mamíferos introducidos, como ratas, ratones, gatos, perros, burros y ganado. Antes había también un gran número de cerdos y cabras introducidos, pero han sido erradicados en los últimos años gracias a las excelentes campañas llevadas a cabo por el Parque Nacional de Galápagos, en colaboración con la Estación Científica Charles Darwin.

Plantas

La flora nativa de las islas Galápagos cuenta con alrededor de 500 especies, de las cuales unas 185 son endémicas. En la actualidad hay unas 800 especies más que han sido introducidas (aunque en muchos casos el número de plantas individuales puede ser pequeño). Como ocurre en el caso de los animales, la evolución se ha manifestado produciendo varios tipos de "radiación adaptativa" entre las plantas. Por ejemplo, la escalesia, un miembro de la familia de las margaritas, cuenta con 21 subespecies, que varían desde pequeños arbustos a árboles, mientras que la chumbera opuntia ha desarrollado 14 subespecies. Las plantas varían mucho en las Galápagos, dependiendo de su hábitat particular, según crezcan, por ejemplo, en zonas costeras, áridas o húmedas.

Mamíferos marinos

Hay dos especies endémicas de mamíferos marinos que acuden hasta la orilla en las Galápagos. Los leones marinos pueden verse a menudo en las playas arenosas, donde se reúnen en harenes en la estación de apareamiento, entre mayo y septiembre. En contraste, la foca peletera de Galápagos es mucho más pequeña y no tan fácil de ver en las orillas rocosas donde descansa durante el día. Los antepasados de la foca peletera debían ser originarios de regiones más frías, mucho más al sur. Además, varios tipos de ballenas y delfines pueden verse en el mar, alrededor de las islas.

Tortugas marinas

La tortuga verde del Pacífico es fácil de ver, sobre todo en la estación de apareamiento, de noviembre a diciembre. Las hembras ponen los huevos por la noche en las playas arenosas, de diciembre a junio. Otras tortugas, como la laúd, la carey y la golfina, pueden verse de vez en cuando pero no crían en las islas.

Otros tipos de vida marina

La fauna y la flora marinas de las Galápagos son tan insólitas e interesantes de estudiar como sus homólogas terrestres. No en vano su hábitat marino ha sido descrito como la zona más interesante del mundo de su tamaño, desde el punto de vista científico. El archipiélago se alza en el cruce de tres importantes corrientes oceánicas y posee una combinación única de especies tropicales, especies de climas templados y otras más típicas de regiones frías. Más del 11% de las especies de peces son endémicas, junto con el 39% de las algas, el 18% de los moluscos y el 45% de los corales. En su conjunto, el nivel de endemismo es de un 20% lo que supone un porcentaje medio muy importante.

Buceo y submarinismo

El submarinismo sólo está permitido cuando se va acompañado de un guía certificado. Sólo se permite la inmersión a buzos experimentados y con licencia. Hay una cámara de descompresión en Puerto Ayora. Sin embargo, el buceo de superficie es muy gratificante y está al alcance de todos. Se recomienda a los visitantes de las islas nadar siempre en compañía de al menos otra persona. Las corrientes no suelen ser un problema y los ataques de los tiburones son prácticamente inexistentes.

Miscelánea

Las islas Galápagos son una provincia de Ecuador y se encuentran a unos mil kilómetros al oeste del continente sudamericano. El ecuador atraviesa la parte norte del archipiélago.

- El punto más alto es la cima del volcán Wolf, con 1.707 m

- Sólo cinco de las islas están habitadas y la mayoría de la gente vive directa o indirectamente del turismo, de la pesca o de la agricultura. Más de la mitad de la población vive en Puerto Ayora, en la isla de Santa Cruz.

- La capital provincial es Puerto Baquerizo Moreno, en la isla de San Cristóbal.

- Las islas tienen 1.350 km de costas, una longitud mayor que la de Ecuador.

- El archipiélago está formado por más de 130 islas e islotes, de los cuales hay 13 islas principales y alrededor de otros 65 islotes, rocas y arrecifes con nombre propio.

- La superficie terrestre total del archipiélago es de 7.882 Km2.

Isabela es la isla más grande, con una superficie de 4.588 km2. Está compuesta de cinco volcanes y parte de un sexto, que en su origen eran islas separadas, pero que con el tiempo acabaron uniéndose con la lava que fluyó por sus laderas.

Conservación ambiental

El Parque Nacional de Galápagos

La primera iniciativa de protección legal de las islas tuvo lugar en 1936, pero éstas no fueron declaradas parque nacional hasta 1959. La superficie total del parque comprende el 96,6% de la superficie del archipiélago, un total de 7.665 km2. La gestión del parque corre a cargo de la Dirección del Parque Nacional de Galápagos, que comenzó a operar en 1968. El parque fue declarado Patrimonio de la Humanidad por la UNESCO en 1978. En 2001 la designación se extendió para cubrir también la reserva marina.

Normas del Parque Nacional

1. No se debe tocar, recoger, ni molestar a ninguna planta o animal, ni a sus restos (conchas, huesos, trozos de madera), o cualquier otro objeto natural.

2. Hay que tener cuidado de no transportar a las islas, ni de una isla a otra, ningún organismo vivo.

3. No llevar comida a las islas deshabitadas.

4. No tocar ni acercarse a los animales.

5. No dar de comer a los animales.

6. No asustar ni sacar a ningún animal de su lugar de descanso, ni de su madriguera o nido.

7. Mantenerse dentro de las zonas designadas para los visitantes.

8. No dejar ningún desecho en las islas ni lanzarlo por la borda de los barcos.

9. No comprar recuerdos ni objetos hechos con plantas o animales de las islas.

10. No desfigurar las rocas.

11. No visitar las islas, a menos que se vaya acompañado de un guía oficial del parque.

12. Limitarse a visitar las zonas aprobadas oficialmente.

13. No dudar en mostrar una actitud ecologista.

La Reserva Marina de Galápagos

La Reserva Marina de Galápagos fue creada en 1986 y comprendía toda la zona marina dentro de una franja de 15 millas náuticas medidas a partir de una línea que se forma al unir los puntos más externos del archipiélago. En marzo de 1998 los límites se extendieron a 40 millas náuticas desde la línea de base. La Reserva Marina de Galápagos (RMG) cubre ahora más de 140.000 km2 y es la segunda reserva marina más grande del mundo, tras la Gran Barrera de Arrecifes de Coral de Australia. La RMG está administrada por la Dirección del Parque Nacional de Galápagos.

La Fundación Charles Darwin

La Fundación Charles Darwin (FCD) fue creada bajo la ley belga en 1959, el mismo año que se creó el Parque Nacional. Su cometido es aconsejar al gobierno de Ecuador en temas de conservación ambiental. Desde el principio estuvo claro que sería necesario contar con una información científica para conservar los ecosistemas del archipiélago, por lo que se construyó en la isla de Santa Cruz la Estación Científica Charles Darwin como brazo operativo del la FCD. Esta organización trabaja en estrecha cooperación con la Dirección del Parque Nacional.

Organizaciones de Amigos de Galápagos

Las siguientes organizaciones son miembros de esta red internacional. Ellos pueden facilitar más información sobre las Galápagos, así como detalles y consejos para ayudar a la protección de esas maravillosas islas.

Fundación Charles Darwin
Puerto Ayora, Isla Santa Cruz
Galápagos
Ecuador
Tel (593) 5 2 2526-146/147
cdrs@fcdarwin.org.ec
www.darwinfoundation.org

Freunde der Galapagos Inseln
c/o Zoo Zurich
Zurichbergstr. 221
8044 Zurich
Switzerland
Tel +41(0) 254 26 70
galapagos@zoo.ch
www.galapagos-ch.org

Charles Darwin Foundation of Canada
55 Avenue Road, Suite 2250
Toronto ON M5L 3L2
Tel +1 416 9644400
garrett@lomltd.com

Friends of Galapagos New Zealand / Australia
PO Box 11-639
Wellington
New Zealand
info@galapagos.org.nz
www.galapagos.org.nz

The Galapagos Darwin Trust
Banque Internationale à Luxembourg
2, Boulevard Royal
L-2953 Luxembourg

Stichting Vrienden van de Galapagos Eilanden

Contact: Ans D. Thurkow-Hartmans
Binnenweg 44
6955 AZ Ellecom
The Netherlands
Tel/Fax: +31 313 421 940
Email: fin.galapagos@planet.nl
Website: www.galapagos.nl

Zoologische Gesellschaft Frankfurt

Contact: Christof Schenck
Alfred-Brehm-Platz 16
60316 Frankfurt
Germany
Tel: +49 (0) 69 43 4460
Fax: +49 (0) 69 43 9348
Email: info@zgf.de
Website: www.zgf.de

Estados Unidos

Galapagos Conservancy
11150 Fairfax Boulevard, Suite 408
Fairfax, Virginia 22030
Tel +1 703 538 6833
darwin@galapagos.org
www.galapagos.org

Reino Unido

Galapagos Conservation Trust
5 Derby Street
London
W1J 7AB
Tel + 44 (0) 20 7629 5049
gct@gct.org
www.savegalapagos.org

Nordic Friends of Galapagos

Contact: Kenneth Kumenius
Korkeasaari
00570 Helsinki
Finland
Tel: +358 50 564 4279
Email: k.kumenius@kolumbus.fi
Website: www.galapagosnordic.fi

The Japan Association for Galapagos (JAGA)

C/o Nature's Planet
3-15-13-403 kita-Aoyama
Minato-ku
Tokyo 107-0061
Japan
Tel/Fax: +81 (0) 3 5766 4060
Email: info@j-galapagos.org
Website: www.j-galapagos.org

General Information

History and settlement

The Galápagos Islands may have been discovered by people of the Chimu culture, and visited by the Inca king Tupac Yupanqui, in the 15th century, but the evidence is inconclusive. The first definitely documented discovery was in 1535, when a ship carrying the Bishop of Panama, Fray Tomás de Berlanga, drifted across to Galápagos on a voyage to Peru. A few years later another group of Spaniards accidentally found the islands. The reports of these two voyages emphasised the harsh appearance of Galápagos, and lack of fresh water, which did not offer much incentive to explore the islands.

The pirate era

Once it became known that there was land out in the Pacific Ocean, and that there were some sources of water, Galápagos soon became the haunt of pirates and buccaneers who intercepted Spanish treasure ships and raided the colonial ports in what is now Peru and Ecuador. They began to use the islands in the late 16th century, and continued to do so until the early 18th century, coming for fuel, water, to repair their ships, and to collect tortoises for meat. Buccaneer Cove, on the northwest of Santiago Island, was a popular anchorage. The pirates were a variety of nationalities, but mainly English and French.

Whalers and sealers

In 1793 and 1794 James Colnett, a British Royal Navy Captain, visited Galápagos during a voyage to assess the whale stocks. He reported huge numbers of whales, which led to a kind of gold rush, as whaling ships started to arrive, first from Britain, then European and American ports. The result was wholesale slaughter, and great wealth for the whalers. In the years 1811-1844 at least 700 American whaling ships were operating in the Pacific. The whalers were soon joined by sealers, whose activities almost made the Galápagos fur seal extinct. One factor helped make this exploitation possible—the apparently unlimited supply of fresh meat in the form of giant tortoises. Some ships loaded as many as 600 tortoises, which could live for up to a year without food or water. The inevitable result was that the carnage only came to an end around 1865 when the whales and seals were too few to be worth hunting. This reprieved the remaining tortoises, but not before the species living on the islands of Floreana, Rábida, and Santa Fé had become extinct.

Early settlements

The first settlement was established on Floreana when Ecuador officially annexed the islands in 1832. This did not get off to a good start and because later arrivals were prisoners it soon became a penal colony. Later attempts at colonisation took place on Floreana, Santa Cruz, southern Isabela, and San Cristóbal, mostly ending in failure or bloodshed. One plantation based at Progreso, on San Cristóbal, was quite successful in harvesting sugar cane, coffee, and other products, but the Manager, Manuel Cobos, treated his employees so badly that they rebelled and killed him in 1904. The last penal colony, on southern Isabela, lasted from 1946-1959, only ending after a mass escape by most of the prisoners.

The search for Utopia

The story of Galápagos settlement has its colourful aspects. In the 1920s and 1930s the world was starting to hear about the islands, and the somewhat romantic newspaper and magazine stories led to a number of "utopia-seekers" making their way to the islands. In 1926, some Norwegians arrived in Floreana to set up a fish canning business. This was not successful. Meanwhile other Norwegians went to Santa Cruz and San Cristóbal. These settlements failed, for various reasons, but some individuals stayed.

Then in 1929, two Germans, a slightly mad philosopher named Friedrich Ritter and his partner Dore Strauch, showed up on Floreana. They were joined in 1932 by two more Germans, Heinz and Margret Wittmer, and later still by a trio comprising an Austrian Baroness and her two lovers. The three groups did not get on well together, and by the end of 1934, only the Wittmers were left, the others having died or disappeared in mysterious circumstances. Margret Wittmer died peacefully in the year 2000, but her son's company, Rolf Wittmer Turismo, offers tourist cruises in the islands.

By contrast, a quiet American couple, Ainslie and Frances Conway, lived on Floreana and Santiago for a year or two before and after World War II, and apparently enjoyed the experience. Other Germans came to Santa Cruz and San Cristóbal Island in the inter-war years, notably the five Angermeyer brothers, whose descendants still live there.

Today, Galápagos has a growing population of Ecuadorians who are active in tourism, agriculture, and fishing.

Natural History

Geological origin

The Galápagos Islands were formed by volcanic activity, and are very young in geological terms, being no more than 10 million years old. They stand near the junction of three huge tectonic plates that are being pushed apart. The Nazca plate, on which Galápagos sits, is moving southeast at a rate of about 7 cm (2.7 inches) a year. According to the "hot spot" theory, the earth's crust in the Galápagos region is moving over a stationary hot spot, causing periodic eruptions which lead to the creation of volcanoes, which become volcanic islands. The oldest are those that are farthest away from the hot spot, such as Española and San Cristóbal, where volcanic activity has ceased. The youngest is Fernandina in the west, which is more or less over the hot spot. Fernandina and neighbouring Isabela are now the most volcanically active parts of the archipelago.

Ocean currents

Several powerful oceanic currents influence the climate and the ecology of Galápagos. Not only do they cause major events like El Niño, but their temperature, direction, and position influence which fishes and other marine life inhabit the islands' waters. This in turn affects any animals that rely on the sea as a food source, such as marine iguanas and sea birds. The South Equatorial Current is the fastest, while the cold Humboldt Current sweeps up from the cooler waters of the south. The system is complex, with counter-currents, such as the Cromwell sub-equatorial counter-current, flowing in unexpected directions, and water at the surface moving differently from water at depth.

Climate

Considering that the islands are located in the tropics, their micro-climate is unusually dry. There are two seasons: hot with short, sharp showers, mainly blue skies and high sea water temperatures from December to June; and cooler and wetter weather (especially in the highlands), with more cloudy skies from June to December. The latter is called the *garúa* season, characterised by winds from the southeast and cooler water brought up by the Humboldt Current. Rainfall varies greatly with altitude, with higher regions receiving more than the lower areas. El Niño years sometimes bring a great increase in rainfall across the islands. However, the air temperature does not vary drastically, despite the difference in the seasons. In March, it can exceed 30°C (86°F), while in August and September, it averages about 22°C (72°F).

El Niño (the Southern Oscillation)

A cool current usually travels westwards from the Galápagos, but every 5-7 years, the southeast trade winds slacken, causing a large volume of warm surface water to surge eastwards to Galápagos and on to South America. Sea water temperatures can rise dramatically, causing storms and heavy rain. Because this invariably happens around Christmas, the event has been given the name El Niño, which means the Christ Child. The sudden climatic change causes changes in the marine environment, resulting in starvation among seabirds and other animals that depend on the sea for food. On land, however, there is profuse vegetation growth, benefiting land birds, reptiles, and insects.

Endemic species

Because Galápagos has never been part of any other land mass, all its animals and plants arrived via a process termed "long-distance dispersal." This means they were carried in the air; transported by the sea (seals and penguins swam, while rice rats and reptiles were carried on rafts of vegetation); or ferried by birds (seeds carried in their gut or attached to their feet or feathers). If the animal or plant survived the journey from the mainland, and was able to survive in Galápagos, its offspring would need to adapt to their new surroundings and compete with other organisms already there. Many Galápagos organisms have been isolated for hundreds or thousands of years, and have grown so different from the parent populations that they are considered new species – or endemic species, which means they are found nowhere else. It is these processes that give Galápagos its reputation as a "laboratory of evolution."

Charles Darwin

The young Darwin was greatly impressed with the diversity of species that he saw in Galápagos on his brief visit in 1835, and this seems to have started the train of thought that finally blossomed in 1859 in his revolutionary book, On the *Origin of Species by Means of Natural Selection*. He hints at this in his book *The Voyage of the Beagle*, when he writes about Galápagos: "Hence, both in space and time, we seem to be brought somewhat near to that great fact, that mystery of mysteries, the first appearance of new beings on this earth."

Wildlife

Seabirds

Situated hundreds or thousands of miles from other land, the Galápagos Islands attract a wide range of breeding seabird species. It has been estimated that there may be three-quarters of a million seabirds here, including significant proportions of some species' populations. There are 19 resident species, of which 5 are endemic, plus some non-breeding migrants and vagrants. Among them are a penguin and an albatross, whose ancestors would have arrived from much colder southern regions. There is a cormorant that cannot fly, the world's only nocturnal gull, the world's rarest gull, the largest red-footed booby colony in the world, and two species of storm petrels that share the same nest site, but one of them is there at night and the other in the daytime.

Coastal birds

This group comprises a variety of herons and egrets, a flamingo, a duck, and various waders and migrants. The list includes one endemic species, the lava gull, and several endemic subspecies. The migrant birds are mainly those that breed in North America, and come south in the northern winter.

Land birds

Most of the small number of land birds in Galápagos are endemic, with 25 of the 30 breeding species or subspecies being found nowhere else. The main bird of prey is the Galápagos hawk, which has an interesting breeding system. Several males may mate with one female and then help in raising the young. This is called cooperative polyandry. Other land birds include a dove, two flycatchers, a cuckoo, a warbler and a tiny rail that is rarely seen although it is not uncommon in the highlands. One most interesting group comprises the four endemic species of mockingbirds, of which only a single species occurs on each of the islands where they are found. And most interesting of all are the 13 sparrow-like species collectively known as Darwin's Finches. Each has a specialised beak shape and feeds on different foods, such as seeds (large or small), insects, flowers, and leaves, etc. Two of them, the woodpecker finch and the now very rare mangrove finch, use twigs as tools to extract food from holes in branches.

Reptiles

While mammals dominate the land fauna in most of the world, in Galápagos it is the reptiles that have that role. Best known and most dramatic are the giant tortoises that once numbered around 250,000 but are now down to around 15,000. There are 11 surviving subspecies or races of these animals, five of them on Isabela Island, five others on five different islands, and one represented by a single male, now residing at the research station on Santa Cruz. He is named Lonesome George. There are three species of land iguanas, and one species of marine iguana that breeds on land but feeds in the sea on algae. In addition, there are seven endemic species of lava lizards, and six endemic species of geckos. Finally, there are several species of small, slender endemic snakes, which are quite common and widespread, but are rarely seen.

Mammals

The only native land mammals in Galápagos are two bats and four species of small rodents. There are a number of introduced land mammals, including rats and house mice, cats and dogs, donkeys, and cattle. There used to be large numbers of introduced pigs and goats. But these have been eradicated in recent years by remarkably successful campaigns by the Galápagos National Park in partnership with the Charles Darwin Research Station

Plants

The native flora of Galápagos totals about 500 species, of which around 185 are endemic. There are now a further 800 or so species that have been introduced (although in many cases the number of individual plants may be small). As with the animal life, evolution has expressed itself by producing a number of "adaptive radiations" among the plants. For example, Scalesia, a member of the daisy family, has 21 different subspecies, ranging from small shrubs to trees, while the prickly pear Opuntia has developed 14 subspecies. The plants in Galápagos vary greatly depending on the particular ecological zone in which they occur, e.g. the coastal, arid, or humid areas.

Marine mammals

There are two endemic marine mammals that come ashore in Galápagos. The sea lions can often be seen on sandy beaches, and gather in harems in the mating season between May and September. By contrast, the Galápagos fur seal is much smaller, and is not so easily seen on the rocky shores where it rests in the daytime. The ancestors of this species would have originated in colder regions much farther south. In addition, there are a number of whales and dolphins that may be seen at sea around the islands.

Turtles

The Pacific green turtle is commonly seen, especially in the mating season from November to December. The females lay their eggs at night on sandy beaches from December to June. Other turtles, such as the leatherback, hawksbill, and olive ridley are seen occasionally, but do not breed in the islands.

Other marine life

The marine fauna and flora of Galápagos are in their way just as unusual and worthy of study as their terrestrial counterparts. Indeed, the marine realm has been described as the most scientifically interesting area of its size in the world. The archipelago sits at the crossroads of three major oceanic current systems, and has a unique combination of tropical species, temperate species, and species more typical of cold regions. Over 11% of the fish species are endemic, along with 39% of the seaweeds, 18% of the molluscs, and 45% of the corals. Overall, the level of endemism is around 20% – an extremely high average figure.

Diving & snorkelling

Diving is only permitted when accompanied by a licensed guide. Only experienced divers with qualifications are allowed to participate. There is a decompression chamber in Puerto Ayora. Snorkelling, however, is very rewarding and anyone can do it. Visitors should always swim with at least one other person. Currents are not usually a problem, and shark attacks are virtually unknown.

Miscellaneous

The Galápagos Islands are about 1,000 km (600 miles) to the west of the South American mainland. The Equator runs though the northern part of the archipelago.

● The highest point is Volcán Wolf at 1,707 m (5,600 feet).

● Only five of the islands are inhabited, and most people make their living either directly or indirectly from tourism, farming, or fishing. More than half the population lives in Puerto Ayora on Isla Santa Cruz.

● The provincial capital is Puerto Baquerizo Moreno on Isla San Cristóbal

● The islands have 1,350 km (837 miles) of coastline, which is more than that of mainland Ecuador.

● The archipelago comprises over 130 islands and islets, with 13 principal islands, and about 65 other named islets, rocks, and reefs.

● The total land area of the archipelago is 7,882 sq km (3,043 square miles).

Isabela is the largest island, with an area of 4,588 sq km (1,771 square miles). It is composed of five volcanoes and part of a sixth. These were once separate islands, but over time became joined together by the lava flowing down their sides.

Conservation

Galápagos National Park

The first legal protection for the islands was initiated in1936, but it was not until 1959 that the Galápagos National Park was formally established. The total area of the Park comprises 96.6% of the land area of the archipelago, a total of 7,665 sq km, or 2,960 square miles. It is managed by the Galápagos National Park Service, which began operations in 1968.

National Park Rules

1. No plant, animal, or their remains (shells, bones, pieces of wood) or other natural objects should be removed or disturbed.

2. Be careful not to transport any live material to the islands, or from island to island.

3. Do not take any food onto the uninhabited islands.

4. Do not touch or handle the animals.

5. Do not feed the animals.

6. Do not startle or chase any animal from its resting or nesting spot.

7. Stay within the areas designated as visitor sites.

8. Do not leave any litter on the islands, or throw any off your boat.

9. Do not buy souvenirs or objects made from plants or animals of the islands.

10. Do not deface the rocks.

11. Do not visit the islands unless accompanied by a licensed National Park Guide.

12. Restrict your visit to officially approved areas.

13. Do not hesitate to show your conservationist attitude.

Galápagos Marine Reserve

The Galápagos Marine Resources Reserve was established in 1986, including all waters within 15 nautical miles of a line joining the outermost points of the archipelago. In March 1998, the boundaries were extended to 40 nautical miles from the baseline. The Galápagos Marine Reserve (GMR) as it is now called, covers over 140,000 square kilometres, or about 54,000 square miles. It is the second largest marine reserve in the world, after the Great Barrier Reef in Australia. The GMR is managed by the Galápagos National Park Service.

Charles Darwin Foundation

The Charles Darwin Foundation (CDF) was established under Belgian law in 1959, the same year that the National Park was created. Its role is to advise the government of Ecuador on conservation. From the beginning it was clear that scientific information would be needed to conserve the archipelago's ecosystems, so the Charles Darwin Research Station was built on Santa Cruz Island as the CDF's operational arm. It works in close cooperation with the National Park Service.

Friends of Galápagos Organisations

The following organisations are members of this international network. They can provide further information about Galápagos, and details of how you can help to protect these wonderful islands.

Charles Darwin Foundation / Fundación Charles Darwin

Puerto Ayora, Santa Cruz Island
Galápagos
Ecuador
Tel (593) 5 2 2526-146/147
cdrs@fcdarwin.org.ec
www.darwinfoundation.org

Charles Darwin Foundation of Canada

55 Avenue Road, Suite 2250
Toronto ON M5L 3L2
Tel +1 416 9644400
garrett@lomltd.com

Freunde der Galapagos Inseln

c/o Zoo Zurich
Zurichbergstr. 221
8044 Zurich
Switzerland
Tel +41(0) 254 26 70
galapagos@zoo.ch
www.galapagos-ch.org

Friends of Galapagos New Zealand / Australia

PO Box 11-639
Wellington
New Zealand
info@galapagos.org.nz
www.galapagos.org.nz

United States

Galapagos Conservancy
11150 Fairfax Boulevard, Suite 408
Fairfax, Virginia 22030
Tel +1 703 538 6833
darwin@galapagos.org
www.galapagos.org

United Kingdom

Galapagos Conservation Trust
5 Derby Street
London
W1J 7AB
Tel + 44 (0) 20 7629 5049
gct@gct.org
www.savegalapagos.org

Nordic Friends of Galapagos

Contact: Kenneth Kumenius
Korkeasaari
00570 Helsinki
Finland
Tel: +358 50 564 4279
Email: k.kumenius@kolumbus.fi
Website: www.galapagosnordic.fi

Stichting Vrienden van de Galapagos Eilanden

Contact: Ans D. Thurkow-Hartmans
Binnenweg 44
6955 AZ Ellecom
The Netherlands
Tel/Fax: +31 313 421 940
Email: fin.galapagos@planet.nl
Website: www.galapagos.nl

The Galapagos Darwin Trust

Banque Internationale à Luxembourg
2, Boulevard Royal
L-2953 Luxembourg

The Japan Association for Galapagos (JAGA)

C/o Nature's Planet
3-15-13-403 kita-Aoyama
Minato-ku
Tokyo 107-0061
Japan
Tel/Fax: +81 (0) 3 5766 4060
Email: info@j-galapagos.org
Website: www.j-galapagos.org

Zoologische Gesellschaft Frankfurt

Contact: Christof Schenck
Alfred-Brehm-Platz 16
60316 Frankfurt
Germany
Tel: +49 (0) 69 43 4460
Fax: +49 (0) 69 43 9348
Email: info@zgf.de
Website: www.zgf.de

Allgemeine Informationen

Geschichte und Besiedlung

Die Galápagos-Inseln wurden möglicherweise von Menschen der Chimú-Kultur entdeckt und im 15. Jahrhundert von dem Inkakönig Tupac Yupanqui besucht, wofür aber keine eindeutigen Belege existieren. Die erste sicher dokumentierte Entdeckung fand im Jahr 1535 statt, als ein Schiff mit dem Bischof von Panama, Fray Tomás de Berlanga, an Bord auf einer Reise nach Peru zu den Galápagos-Inseln hinübertrieb. Einige Jahre später fand eine andere Gruppe von Spaniern zufällig die Inseln. Die Berichte von diesen beiden Reisen betonten das unwirtliche Erscheinungsbild von Galápagos sowie den Mangel an Süßwasser und boten damit keinen großen Anreiz zur Erforschung der Inseln.

Das Zeitalter der Piraten

Als bekannt wurde, dass es draußen im Pazifik Land gab und dort auch einige Wasserquellen existierten, wurden die Galápagos-Inseln bald zum Schlupfwinkel für Piraten und Freibeuter, die spanische Schatzschiffe abfingen und die Kolonialhäfen im heutigen Peru und Ecuador überfielen. Sie begannen im späten 16. Jahrhundert mit der Nutzung der Inseln und blieben dort bis ins frühe 18. Jahrhundert. Sie kamen wegen Brennstoff, Wasser, um ihre Schiffe zu reparieren und um Schildkröten wegen ihres Fleisches zu fangen. Buccaneer Cove im Nordwesten von Santiago Island war ein beliebter Ankerplatz. Die Piraten stammten aus vielen verschiedenen Ländern, aber vorwiegend waren es Engländer und Franzosen.

Wal- und Robbenfänger

1793 und 1794 besuchte James Colnett, ein Kapitän der Königlich Britischen Marine, auf einer Reise die Galápagos-Inseln, um den Walbestand zu beurteilen. Er meldete riesige Mengen an Walen, was eine Art Goldrausch auslöste, und es kamen immer mehr Walfangschiffe, zuerst aus Großbritannien, dann aus europäischen und amerikanischen Häfen. Das Ergebnis war eine Massenabschlachtung der Wale und großer Reichtum für die Walfänger. In den Jahren 1811-1844 fuhren mindestens 700 amerikanische Walfänger im Pazifik. Zu den Walfängern stießen bald die Robbenfänger, durch die die Galápagos-Fellrobben beinahe ausgerottet wurden. Ein Umstand trug grundlegend zu dieser Ausbeutung bei – der anscheinend unbegrenzte Vorrat an frischem Fleisch in Form von Riesenschildkröten. Manche Schiffe nahmen bis zu 600 Schildkröten an Bord, die bis zu einem Jahr ohne Futter und Wasser überleben konnten. Das unvermeidliche Ergebnis war, dass das Gemetzel erst um 1865 ein Ende fand, als zu wenig Wale und Robben für einen profitablen Fang übriggeblieben waren. Dadurch wurden die verbleibenden Schildkröten verschont, aber die auf den Inseln Floreana, Rábida und Santa Fé lebenden Arten waren zu diesem Zeitpunkt bereits ausgerottet.

Frühe Besiedlungen

Die erste Siedlung entstand auf Floreana, als Ecuador 1832 die Inseln offiziell annektierte. Es war kein guter Anfang, und weil spätere Ankömmlinge Gefangene waren, wurde daraus bald eine Strafkolonie. Spätere Versuche der Kolonialisierung wurden auf Floreana und Santa Cruz, im Süden von Isabela und auf San Cristóbal unternommen und endeten meist als Misserfolg oder Blutbad. Eine Plantage bei Progreso auf San Cristóbal war recht erfolgreich mit dem Anbau von Zuckerrohr, Kaffee und anderen Produkten, aber der Verwalter, Manuel Cobos, behandelte seine Angestellten so schlecht, dass sie rebellierten und ihn 1904 töteten. Die letzte Strafkolonie im Süden von Isabela bestand von 1946 bis 1959 und fand ihr Ende in einer Massenflucht der meisten Gefangenen.

Die Suche nach Utopia

Die Geschichte der Besiedlung der Galápagos-Inseln hat ihre schillernden Facetten. In den 1920er und 1930er Jahren wurde die Welt langsam auf die Inseln aufmerksam, und die etwas romantischen Zeitungs- und Zeitschriftenartikel führten dazu, dass eine Reihe von Menschen sich auf der Suche nach „Utopia" auf den Weg zu den Inseln machte. 1926 kamen einige Norweger nach Floreana, um eine Fischkonservenfabrik zu errichten. Diese hatte keinen Erfolg. In der Zwischenzeit gingen andere Norweger nach Santa Cruz und San Cristóbal. Diese Siedlungen waren aus verschiedenen Gründen ebenfalls ein Fehlschlag, aber ein paar Menschen blieben.

1929 tauchten dann zwei Deutsche auf Floreana auf: ein leicht verrückter Philosoph namens Friedrich Ritter und seine Partnerin, Dore Strauch. 1932 gesellten sich zwei weitere Deutsche, Heinz und Margret Wittmer, zu ihnen und noch etwas später ein Trio, das aus einer österreichischen Baroness und ihren beiden Liebhabern bestand. Die drei Gruppen kamen nicht gut miteinander aus, und Ende 1934 waren nur noch die Wittmers übrig. Die anderen waren gestorben oder unter mysteriösen Umständen verschwunden. Margret Wittmer verstarb friedlich im Jahr 2000, aber die Firma ihres Sohnes, Rolf Wittmer Turismo, bietet heute Inseltouren für Touristen an.

Im Gegensatz dazu lebte ein ruhiges amerikanische Paar, Ainslie und Frances Conway, ein oder zwei Jahre vor und nach dem 2. Weltkrieg auf Floreana und Santiago, wo es ihnen anscheinend gut gefiel. Weitere Deutsche kamen in den Zwischenkriegsjahren nach Santa Cruz und San Cristóbal, insbesondere die fünf Angermeyer-Brüder, deren Nachkommen noch heute dort leben.

Heute findet sich auf Galápagos eine wachsende Bevölkerung von Ecuadorianern, die im Tourismus, der Landwirtschaft und dem Fischfang tätig sind.

Naturgeschichte

Geologischer Ursprung

Die Galápagos-Inseln sind vulkanischen Ursprungs und geologisch gesehen sehr jung, da sie nicht älter als 10 Millionen Jahre sind. Sie liegen in der Nähe der Verbindungsstelle von drei riesigen tektonischen Platten, die auseinandergedrückt werden. Die Nazca-Platte, auf der die Galápagos-Inseln liegen, bewegt sich mit einer Geschwindigkeit von etwa 7 cm pro Jahr in südöstlicher Richtung. Gemäß der „Hotspot"-Theorie bewegt sich die Erdkruste in der Galápagos-Region über einen feststehenden Hotspot, was regelmäßig Eruptionen verursacht, die zur Entstehung von Vulkanen führen, die wiederum zu Vulkaninseln werden. Die ältesten sind die am weitesten vom Hotspot entfernt liegenden, wie z.b. Española und San Cristóbal, wo die Vulkantätigkeit zum Erliegen gekommen ist. Die jüngste ist Fernandina im Westen, die sich mehr oder weniger direkt über dem Hotspot befindet. Fernandina und die Nachbarinsel Isabela sind heute die Teile des Archipels mit der stärksten Vulkantätigkeit.

Ozeanströmungen

Mehrere starke Ozeanströmungen beeinflussen das Klima und die Ökologie der Galápagos-Inseln. Sie verursachen nicht nur Großereignisse wie z.B. El Niño, sondern ihre Temperatur, Richtung und Position beeinflussen, welche Fische und andere Meereslebewesen die Inselgewässer bewohnen. Dies wiederum wirkt sich auf alle Tiere aus, die auf das Meer als Nahrungsquelle angewiesen sind, wie z.B. Meerechsen und Meeresvögel. Der Südäquatorialstrom ist der schnellste, während der kalte Humboldtstrom aus den kühleren Gewässern im Süden kommt. Es ist ein komplexes System mit Gegenströmungen wie dem subäquatorialen Cromwell-Strom, der in unvorhergesehene Richtungen fließt, und Wasser, das sich an der Oberfläche anders als in der Tiefe bewegt.

Klima

In Anbetracht der Tatsache, dass die Inseln in den Tropen liegen, ist ihr Mikroklima ungewöhnlich trocken. Es gibt zwei Jahreszeiten: Hitze mit kurzen, starken Regenfällen, vorwiegend blauem Himmel und hohen Meerwassertemperaturen von Dezember bis Juni; und kühleres und feuchteres Wetter (vor allem in den Höhenlagen) mit mehr Bewölkung von Juni bis Dezember. Letztere wird die Garúa-Jahreszeit genannt, die von Winden aus Südosten und kühlerem Wasser aus dem Humboldtstrom gekennzeichnet ist. Die Regenfälle hängen sehr von der Höhenlage ab, wobei in den höheren Regionen mehr Regen fällt als in den tiefer liegenden Bereichen. El-Niño-Jahre bringen manchmal eine starke Zunahme der

Regenfälle über den Inseln mit sich. Die Lufttemperatur ändert sich jedoch trotz der unterschiedlichen Jahreszeiten nur geringfügig. Im März kann sie 30 °C übersteigen, während sie im August und September im Durchschnitt bei etwa 22 °C liegt.

El Niño (die südliche Oszillation)

Normalerweise bewegt sich eine kühle Strömung von den Galápagos-Inseln westwärts. Alle 5 – 7 Jahre lassen jedoch die Südost-Passatwinde nach, was dazu führt, dass eine große Menge warmes Oberflächenwasser ostwärts zu den Galápagos-Inseln und weiter nach Südamerika fließt. Die Meerwassertemperaturen können drastisch ansteigen und Stürme und starke Regenfälle hervorrufen. Weil dies ausnahmslos um Weihnachten herum passiert, hat man das Ereignis El Niño getauft, was Christkind bedeutet. Der plötzliche Klimawandel verursacht Veränderungen in der Meeresumwelt, die ein Verhungern unter Meeresvögeln und anderen sich aus dem Meer ernährenden Tieren zur Folge haben. An Land jedoch findet ein üppiges Wachstum der Vegetation statt, wovon Landvögel, Reptilien und Insekten profitieren.

Endemische Arten

Da die Galápagos-Inseln niemals Teil einer anderen Landmasse waren, kamen alle dort heimischen Pflanzen und Tiere über einen Weg dorthin, der als „Fernausbreitung" bezeichnet wird. Das heißt, sie wurden durch die Luft getragen, vom Meer befördert (Robben und Pinguine schwammen, während Reisratten und Reptilien auf Pflanzenflößen getragen wurden) oder von Vögeln transportiert (Samen im Darm oder an den Füßen oder Federn). Wenn das Tier oder die Pflanze die Reise vom Festland überlebte und in der Lage war, auf Galápagos zu überleben, mussten die Nachkommen sich ihrer neuen Umgebung anpassen und mit bereits vorhandenen Organismen konkurrieren. Viele Galápagos-Organismen sind seit Hunderten oder Tausenden von Jahren isoliert und haben sich so unterschiedlich von den Ursprungspopulationen weiterentwickelt, dass sie als neue oder endemische Arten angesehen werden, was bedeutet, dass sie nirgendwo sonst zu finden sind. Es sind diese Vorgänge, die den Galápagos-Inseln ihren Ruf als „Evolutionslabor" verliehen haben.

Charles Darwin

Der junge Darwin war tief beeindruckt von der Artenvielfalt, die er bei seinem kurzen Besuch im Jahre 1835 auf den Galápagos-Inseln antraf. Es scheint, als habe dies den Gedankengang angeregt, der schließlich 1859 in seinem revolutionären Buch „Über die Entstehung der Arten durch natürliche Zuchtwahl" zur Entfaltung kam. In seinem Buch „Die Fahrt der Beagle" weist er darauf hin, wenn er über die Galápagos-Inseln schreibt: „Daher scheint es, dass wir in Raum und Zeit etwas näher an diese bedeutende Tatsache, dieses Wunder der Wunder, das erste Erscheinen neuer Wesen auf der Erde herangeführt werden."

Fauna und Flora

Meeresvögel

Durch ihre Lage Hunderte oder Tausende Meilen von anderen Landmassen entfernt, ziehen die Galápagos-Inseln ein große Vielzahl brütender Meeresvogelarten an. Es wird geschätzt, dass es hier bis zu einer dreiviertel Million Meeresvögel gibt, einschließlich bedeutender Anteile mancher Artenbestände. Es gibt 19 heimische Arten, von denen 5 endemisch sind, zuzüglich einiger nicht-brütender Zugvögel und nicht-sesshafter Vögel. Dazu gehören ein Pinguin und ein Albatros, deren Vorfahren aus viel kälteren südlichen Regionen gekommen sein müssen. Es gibt einen Kormoran, der nicht fliegen kann, die einzige Nachtmöwe der Welt, die seltenste Möwe der Welt, die größte Kolonie von Rotfußtölpeln der Welt und zwei Arten von Sturmschwalben, die dasselbe Nest teilen, aber eine ist nachts dort und die andere am Tag.

Küstenvögel

Diese Gruppe umfasst eine Vielfalt an Reihern, einen Flamingo, eine Ente und diverse Sumpf- und Zugvögel. Die Liste schließt auch eine endemische Art ein, die Lavamöwe, sowie einige endemische Unterarten. Die Zugvögel sind hauptsächlich jene, die in Nordamerika brüten und im nördlichen Winter nach Süden fliegen.

Landvögel

Die meisten der wenigen Landvögel auf Galápagos sind endemisch, wobei 25 der 30 brütenden Arten oder Unterarten nirgendwo sonst vorkommen. Der wichtigste Raubvogel ist der Galápagosfalke, der eine interessante Brutgewohnheit hat. Mehrere Männchen können sich mit einem Weibchen paaren und dann dabei helfen, die Jungen aufzuziehen. Dies nennt man kooperative Polyandrie. Zu den anderen Landvögeln gehören eine Taube, zwei Fliegenschnäpper, ein Kuckuck, ein Goldwaldsänger und eine winzige Ralle, die man nur selten sieht, obwohl sie im Gebirge nicht selten ist. Eine sehr interessante Gruppe umfasst die vier endemischen Arten von Spottdrosseln, wobei nur eine einzige Art auf der jeweiligen Insel vorkommt, auf der man sie findet. Am interessantesten aber sind die 13 spatzenartigen Gattungen, die unter dem Sammelbegriff „Darwinfinken" bekannt sind. Jede Art hat ihre besondere Schnabelform und ernährt sich von unterschiedlicher Nahrung, wie z.B. Samenkörnern (groß oder klein), Insekten, Blumen, Blättern usw. Zwei davon, der Spechtfink und der heute sehr seltene Mangrove-Darwinfink, verwenden Zweige als Werkzeug, um Futter aus Astlöchern zu holen.

Reptilien

Während Säugetiere fast auf der ganzen Welt in der Landfauna überwiegen, fällt diese Rolle auf den Galápagos-Inseln den Reptilien zu. Am bekanntesten und aufregendsten sind die Riesenschildkröten, die einst um die 250.000 zählten, jetzt aber auf ungefähr 15.000 zurückgegangen sind. Es gibt 11 überlebende Unterarten oder Rassen dieser Tiere, fünf davon auf Isabela Island, fünf weitere auf fünf verschiedenen Inseln und eine, die durch ein einziges Männchen vertreten wird, das heute in der Forschungsstation auf Santa Cruz lebt. Es heißt „Lonesome George" (einsamer George). Es gibt drei Arten von Landleguanen und eine Meeresleguanart, die an Land brütet, sich aber mit Algen aus dem Meer ernährt. Darüber hinaus gibt es sieben endemische Arten von Lavaeidechsen und sechs endemische Arten von Geckos. Schließlich gibt es noch mehrere Arten kleiner, dünner endemischer Schlangen, die häufig vorkommen und weitverbreitet sind, aber kaum gesehen werden.

Säugetiere

Die einzigen einheimischen Landsäugetiere auf Galápagos sind zwei Fledermäuse und vier Arten kleiner Nagetiere. Es gibt eine Reihe von eingeführten Landsäugetieren, einschließlich Ratten und Hausmäuse, Katzen und Hunde, Esel und Rinder. Es gab auch einmal eine große Anzahl an eingeführten Schweinen und Ziegen. Diese wurden aber in den letzten Jahren durch außergewöhnlich erfolgreiche Aktionen des Galápagos Nationalparks in Zusammenarbeit mit der Charles-Darwin-Forschungsstation stark reduziert, wenn nicht gar gänzlich beseitigt.

Pflanzen

Die heimische Flora der Galápagos-Inseln beläuft sich auf etwa 500 Arten, von denen ca. 175 endemisch sind. Heute gibt es ungefähr weitere 550 Arten, die eingeführt wurden (obwohl in manchen Fällen die Anzahl der einzelnen Pflanzen gering sein kann). Wie auch in der Tierwelt hat sich die Evolution in einer Reihe von „anpassungsfähigen Ausbreitungen" unter den Pflanzen gezeigt. So hat z.B. Scalesia, ein Mitglied der Gänseblümchenfamilie, 21 verschiedene Unterarten, die von kleinen Stauden bis hin zu Bäumen reichen, während die Kaktusfeige Opuntia 14 Unterarten entwickelt hat. Die Pflanzen auf Galápagos unterscheiden sich sehr stark, abhängig von dem jeweiligen ökologischen Gebiet, in dem sie auftreten, z.B. in Küsten-, Trocken- oder Feuchtgebieten.

Meeressäugetiere

Es gibt zwei endemische Meeressäugetiere, die auf den Galápagos-Inseln an Land gehen. In sandigen Buchten kann man oft die Seelöwen beobachten, die sich in der Paarungszeit zwischen Mai und September in Harems versammeln. Dagegen ist die Galápagos-Fellrobbe viel kleiner und ist auf den steinigen Küsten, wo sie sich tagsüber ausruht, nicht so leicht zu entdecken. Die Vorfahren dieser Art stammen wohl aus kühleren Regionen viel weiter südlich. Darüber hinaus gibt es eine Reihe von Walen und Delfinen, die man im Meer um die Inseln herum entdecken kann.

Schildkröten

Die grüne Wasserschildkröte ist häufig zu sehen, besonders in der Paarungszeit von November bis Dezember. Von Dezember bis Juni legen die Weibchen nachts ihre Eier auf Sandstränden ab. Gelegentlich sieht man andere Schildkrötenarten wie z.B. die Lederrücken-, die echte Karett- und die Oliv-Bastardschildkröte, diese brüten aber nicht auf den Inseln.

Andere Meereslebewesen

Die Meeresfauna und -flora der Galápagos-Inseln sind auf ihre Weise genauso ungewöhnlich und untersuchenswert wie ihre terrestrischen Gegenstücke. So wurden die hiesigen Meeresgefilde als die wissenschaftlich interessanteste Region dieser Größe auf der Welt beschrieben. Der Archipel liegt an der Kreuzung von drei großen Meeresströmungen und besitzt eine einzigartige Kombination von tropischen Arten, Arten der gemäßigten Zone und Arten, die eher typisch für kalte Regionen sind. Mehr als 11 % der Fischarten sind endemisch, daneben 39 % der Meeresalgen, 18 % der Weichtiere und 45 % der Korallen. Insgesamt liegt der Grad an Endemismus bei ungefähr 20 % – ein äußerst hoher Durchschnittswert.

Tauchen und Schnorcheln

Tauchen ist ausschließlich in Begleitung eines zugelassenen Führers erlaubt. In Puerto Ayora gibt es eine Dekompressionskammer. Es gibt auf den Galápagos-Inseln keine Dekompressionskammer. Schnorcheln hingegen lohnt sich sehr und ist allgemein erlaubt. Besucher sollten immer mit mindestens einer weiteren Person zusammen schwimmen. Strömungen sind meistens kein Problem und Angriffe von Haien sind so gut wie nicht bekannt.

Verschiedenes

Die Galápagos-Inseln liegen ca. 1.000 km westlich vom südamerikanischen Festland. Der Äquator verläuft durch den nördlichen Teil des Archipels.

● Die höchste Erhebung ist der Volcán Wolf mit 1.707 m.

● Nur fünf der Inseln sind bewohnt, und die meisten Menschen leben entweder direkt oder indirekt vom Tourismus, von der Landwirtschaft oder der Fischerei. Über die Hälfte der Bevölkerung lebt in Puerto Ayora auf der Insel Santa Cruz.

● Die Provinzhauptstadt ist Puerto Baquerizo Moreno auf der Insel San Cristóbal.

- Die Inseln haben eine 1.350 km lange Küste, länger als jene von Ecuador auf dem Festland.

- Der Archipel umfasst mehr als 130 Inseln und Inselchen mit 13 Hauptinseln und etwa 65 anderen Inselchen, Felsen und Riffen, die alle einen Namen tragen.

- Die gesamte Landfläche des Archipels beträgt 7.882 km^2.

Isabela ist die größte Insel mit einer Fläche von 4.588 km^2. Sie besteht aus fünf Vulkanen und dem Teil eines sechsten. Dies waren einmal separate Inseln, wurden aber mit der Zeit durch die an ihren Seiten herunterfließende Lava verbunden.

Naturschutz

Galápagos Nationalpark

Der erste gesetzliche Schutz für die Inseln wurde 1936 ins Leben gerufen, aber erst 1959 wurden sie offiziell zum Galápagos Nationalpark erklärt. Die Gesamtfläche des Parks umfasst 96,6 % der Landfläche des Archipels, insgesamt 7.665 km². Er wird vom Galápagos National Park Service verwaltet, der 1968 seine Arbeit aufnahm.

Regeln für den Nationalpark

1. Keine Pflanzen, keine Tiere oder deren Überreste (Muscheln, Knochen, Holzstücke) und keine anderen natürlichen Objekte dürfen entfernt oder gestört werden.

2. Achten Sie darauf, kein lebendes Material auf die Inseln oder von einer Insel zur anderen mitzunehmen.

3. Bringen Sie keine Lebensmittel auf die unbewohnten Inseln.

4. Tiere dürfen nicht angefasst oder bewegt werden.

5. Tiere dürfen nicht gefüttert werden.

6. Tiere dürfen nicht von ihren Ruhe- und Nistplätzen aufgescheucht oder vertrieben werden.

7. Bleiben Sie in den für Besucher gekennzeichneten Bereichen.

8. Es darf kein Abfall auf den Inseln zurückgelassen oder über Bord geworfen werden.

9. Kaufen Sie keine Souvenirs oder Gegenstände, die aus Pflanzen oder Tieren von der Insel hergestellt wurden.

10. Die Felsen dürfen nicht verunstaltet werden.

11. Besuchen Sie die Inseln nur in Begleitung eines zugelassenen Nationalpark-Führers.

12. Beschränken Sie Ihren Besuch auf offiziell zugelassene Bereiche.

13. Zögern Sie nicht, Ihre Haltung als Naturschützer zum Ausdruck zu bringen.

Galápagos Meeresreservat

Das „Galápagos Marine Resources Reserve" wurde 1986 gegründet und umfasst alle Gewässer innerhalb von 15 Seemeilen einer Linie, die die äußersten Punkte des Archipels verbindet. Im März 1998 wurden die Grenzen auf 40 Seemeilen von der Grundlinie erweitert. Das Galápagos Marine Reserve (GMR), wie es heute heißt, erstreckt sich über mehr als 140.000 Quadratkilometer. Es ist nach dem Great Barrier Reef in Australien das zweitgrößte Meeresreservat der Welt. Das GMR wird vom Galápagos National Park Service verwaltet.

Charles Darwin Foundation

Die Charles Darwin Foundation (CDF) wurde 1959 nach belgischem Gesetz gegründet, im selben Jahr, als der Nationalpark geschaffen wurde. Ihre Aufgabe ist es, die Regierung von Ecuador in Sachen Naturschutz zu beraten. Es war von Anfang an klar, dass wissenschaftliche Informationen erforderlich sein würden, um das Ökosystem des Archipels zu schützen. So wurde die Charles Darwin Forschungsstation auf der Insel Santa Cruz gebaut, als ausführende Instanz der CDF. Sie arbeitet eng mit dem National Park Service zusammen.

Organisationen der Freunde von Galápagos

Folgende Organisationen sind Mitglieder dieses internationalen Netzwerks. Sie können weitere Informationen über die Galápagos-Inseln zur Verfügung stellen sowie Einzelheiten darüber, wie Sie helfen können, diese wundervollen Inseln zu schützen.

Charles Darwin Foundation / Fundación Charles Darwin
Puerto Ayora, Santa Cruz Island
Galápagos
Ecuador
Tel. (593) 5 2 2526-146/147
cdrs@fcdarwin.org.ec
www.darwinfoundation.org

Charles Darwin Foundation of Canada
55 Avenue Road, Suite 2250
Toronto ON M5L 3L2
Tel. +1 416 9644400
garrett@lomltd.com

Freunde der Galápagos Inseln
c/o Zoo Zürich
Zürichbergstr. 221
8044 Zürich
Schweiz
Tel +41(0) 254 26 70
Galápagos@zoo.ch
www.Galápagos-ch.org

Friends of Galápagos New Zealand / Australia
PO Box 11-639
Wellington
Neuseeland
info@Galápagos.org.nz
www.Galápagos.org.nz

U.S.A.

Galápagos Conservancy
11150 Fairfax Boulevard, Suite 408
Fairfax, Virginia 22030
Tel. +1 703 538 6833
darwin@Galápagos.org
www.Galápagos.org

Zoologische Gesellschaft Frankfurt

Contact: Christof Schenck
Alfred-Brehm-Platz 16
60316 Frankfurt
Germany
Tel: +49 (0) 69 43 4460
Fax: +49 (0) 69 43 9348
Email: info@zgf.de
Website: www.zgf.de

Nordic Friends of Galapagos

Contact: Kenneth Kumenius
Korkeasaari
00570 Helsinki
Finland
Tel: +358 50 564 4279
Email: k.kumenius@kolumbus.fi
Website: www.galapagosnordic.fi

The Galapagos Darwin Trust

Banque Internationale à Luxembourg
2, Boulevard Royal
L-2953 Luxembourg

Großbritannien

Galápagos Conservation Trust
5 Derby Street
London
W1J 7AB
Tel. + 44 (0) 20 7629 5049
gct@gct.org
www.saveGalápagos.org

Stichting Vrienden van de Galapagos Eilanden

Contact: Ans D. Thurkow-Hartmans
Binnenweg 44
6955 AZ Ellecom
The Netherlands
Tel/Fax: +31 313 421 940
Email: fin.galapagos@planet.nl
Website: www.galapagos.nl

The Japan Association for Galapagos (JAGA)

C/o Nature's Planet
3-15-13-403 kita-Aoyama
Minato-ku
Tokyo 107-0061
Japan
Tel/Fax: +81 (0) 3 5766 4060
Email: info@j-galapagos.org
Website: www.j-galapagos.org

BIBLIOGRAFÍA

BIBLIOGRAPHY

LITERATURVERZEICHNIS

Dickinson, E C. (Editor) The Howard and Moore Complete Checklist of the Birds of the World, Third Edition, Christopher Helm, 2003.

Fitter, J, Fitter, D, and Hosking, D. Wildlife of the Galapagos, HarperCollins, 2000.

Harris, M. Birds of Galapagos, HarperCollins, 1992.

Hickman J. The Enchanted Islands: The Galapagos Discovered, Anthony Nelson, 1991.

Jackson, Michael H. Galápagos: Una Historia Natural. University of Calgary Press, 1997.

McMullen, C K. Flowering Plants of the Galápagos, Cornell University Press, 1999.

Merlen, G. Guia de los Mamiferos Marinos de Galápagos / A Field Guide to the Marine Mammals of Galápagos, Privately printed in Ecuador.

Perry, R. (Editor). Key Environments: Galapagos, Pergamon Press for IUCN, 1984.

Swash, A. and Still, Rob. Birds, Mammals and Reptiles of the Galápagos Islands, Christopher Helm, 2005.

Thornton, I. Darwin's Islands: A Natural History of the Galápagos, The Natural History Press for The American Museum of Natural History, 1971

ÍNDICE

Acacia 72
Aguila Pescadora 24
Albatros de Galápagos 2
Algodón de Galápagos 74
Amargo 76
Arrayancillo 70

Ballena Piloto 48
Ballena de Bryde 46
Ballena Minke 46
Ballena Jorobada 46
Ballena Azul 46
Ballena Sei 46
Blechnum polypodioides 86
Blechnum occidentale 86

Cacaotillo 82
Cachalote 46
Cacto Candelabro 70
Cacto de Lava 70
Cafeto 80
Canario Maria 28
Cerceta Aliazul 16
Chala 72
Chamaesyce 76
Chorlitejo 18
Chorlitejo Semipalmado 22
Chorlito de Rompientes 22
Cormorán no Volador 8
Correlino 22
Ctenitis sloanei 86
Cuclillo 26
Cucuve de Galápagos 30
Cucuve de Española
Cucuve de San Cristóbal 30
Cucuve de Floreana 30
Cyperus 76

Darwiniothamnus 74
Delfin Mular 48
Delfin Comœn 48
Delfin Gris 48

Errante 18
Espino 74

Falaropo de Wilson 18
Falaropo Norteño 18
Falsa Orca 48
Flamboyán 72
Flamenco mayor 16
Flor de la pasión 74
Fragata Común 8
Fragata Real 8
Frambuesa 82

Gallareta Frentirroja 26
Garcita Estriada 14
Garcita Blanca 14
Garrapatero 26
Garza Morena 14
Garza de Lava 14
Garza Vaquera 14
Garza Blanca 14
Gavilán de Galápagos 24
Gaviota de Cola Bifurcada 10
Gaviota de Franklin 10
Gaviota de Lava 10
Gaviotín Rea 10
Gaviotín Tiznado 10
Golondrina de Horquilla 28
Golondrina de Iglesias 28
Golondrina de Galápagos 28
Gonatodes caudiscutatus 58
Gran Pinzón Arbóreo 34
Gran Pinzón Terrestre 32
Gran Pinzón de Cacto 32
Guayabillo 80

Halcón Peregrino 24
Helecho arbóreo 82
Huaque o Garza Nocturna 14
Huaycundu 80

Iguana Terrestre de Santa Fé 60
Iguana Terrestre Rosada 60
Iguana Terrestre 60
Ipomoea 66

Lagartija de lava de Galápagos
  56
Lagartija de lava de Española 56
Lagartija de lava de San Cristóbal
  56
Lantana de Galápagos 76
Lechoso 80
Lechuza Blanca 24
Lechuza de Campo 24
Lecocarpus 76
Lepidodactylus lugrubris 58
Lobo Peletero de Galápagos 44
Lobo Marino de Galápagos 44
Lycopodiella 82

Mangle Negro 64
Mangle Blanco 64
Mangle Rojo 64
Mangle Botón 64
Manzanillo 72
Matazarno 70
Mediano Pinzón Terrestre 32
Mediano Pinzón Arbóreo 34
Monte Colorado 76
Monte Salado 66
Muérdago de Galápagos 80
Murciélago Vespertino
  Galápagueño 40
Murciélago Escarchado 40
Muyuyo 72

Nephrolepis pectinata 86
Nodi o Gaviotín Pardo 10
Nolana 66

Orca 48
Orquídea de Galápagos 80

Ostrero 16
Pachay 26
Pájaro Tropical o Piloto 6
Pájaro Brujo 28
Palo Verde 72
Palo Santo 70
Paloma Bravía 26
Paloma de Galápagos 26
Papamoscas de Galápagos 28
Patillo 16
Pelícano Café 8
Pequeño Pinzón Terrestre 32
Pequeño Pinzón Arbóreo 34
Petrel de Leach 4
Petrel Patapegada 4
Petrel de Madeira 4
Petrel de Elliot 4
Petrel de Galápagos 4
Phyllodactlyus bauri 58
Phyllodactylus reissi 58
Phyllodactylus galapagoensis 58
Pingüino de Galápagos 2
Pinzón Vegetariano 34
Pinzón Terrestre de Pico Agudo 32
Pinzón de Cacto 32

Pinzón Cantor 34
Pinzón Carpintero 34
Pinzón de Manglar 34
Piquero de Nazca 6
Piquero de Patas Rojas 6
Piquero de Patas Azules 6
Playero Común 22
Playero Cabezón 22
Playero Enano 22
Polygala 66
Polypodium tridens 86
Portulaca 66
Pteridium 82
Pufino de Galápagos 2
Pufino Negro 4

Quinina roja 82

Rata Pequeño de Fernandina 40
Rata Gran de Fernandina 40
Rata Endémica de Galápagos 40
Rata de Santiago 40

Satsola 66
Scalesia affinis 84
Scalesia villosa 84

Scalesia helleri 84
Scalesia stewartii 84
Scalesia atractyloides 84
Scalesia crockeri 84
Serpiente de Floreana 54
Serpiente de Española 54
Serpiente de Isabela 54
Serpiente de Steindachner 54
Serpiente de Steindachner 54
Sesuvium 66

Tero Real 18
Thelypteris oligocarpa 86
Tiquilia 76
Tomatillo de Galápagos 74
Tordo Arrocero 30
Tortuga Carey 52
Tortuga Negra 52
Tortuga Gigante de las Galápagos 52
Tuna 70
Uva de Playa 66
Vulvepiedras 22
Waltheria 74
Zarapito 18
Zifio Comœn 48

INDEX

Acacia 72
American Flamingo 16
American Oystercatcher 16
Anderson's Sedge 76

Barn Swallow 28
Barn Owl 24
Baur's Leaf-toed Gecko 58
Beach Morning Glory 66
Bitterbush 76
Black Mangrove 64
Black-necked Stilt 18
Blue Whale 46
Blue-footed Booby 6
Blue-winged Teal 16
Bobolink 30
Bottle-nose Dolphin 48
Bracken 82
Brown Pelican 8
Brown Noddy 10
Bryde's Whale 46
Button Mangrove 64

Cactus Finch 32
Candelabra Cactus 70
Cattle Egret 14
Chamaesyce 76
Coffee 80
Crocker's Scalesia 84
Cuvier's Beaked Whale 48

Dark-billed Cuckoo 26

Elliot's (White-vented) Storm
   Petrel 4
Española Lava Lizard 56
Española Snake 54
Española Mockingbird 30

False Killer Whale 48
Flamboyant 72
Flightless Cormorant 8

Floreana Mockingbird 30
Floreana Snake 54
Florida lace fern 86
Franklin's Gull 10

Galápagos Mistletoe 80
Galápagos Bromeliad 80
Galápagos Guava 80
Galápagos Lantana 76
Galápagos Rail 26
Galápagos Land Iguana 60
Galápagos Orchid 80
Galápagos Hawk 24
Galápagos Dove 26
Galápagos Carpetweed 66
Galápagos Penguin 2
Galápagos Tree Fern 82
Galápagos Tomato 74
Galápagos Flycatcher 28
Galápagos Cotton 74
Galápagos Martin 28
Galápagos (Wedge-rumped)
   Storm Petrel 4
Galápagos Lava Lizard 56
Galápagos Mockingbird 30
Galápagos Giant Tortoise 52
Galápagos Croton 72
Galápagos Miconia 82
Galápagos Leaf-toed Gecko 58
Galápagos Fur Seal 44
Galápagos Sea Lion 44
Galápagos Clubleaf 66
Galápagos Red Bat 40
Galápagos Rice Rat 40
Galápagos Petrel 4
Galápagos Purslane 66
Galápagos Shearwater 2
Galápagos Club Moss 82
Great Blue Heron 14
Great Frigatebird 8
Great Egret 14
Green Turtle 52

Grey (Black-bellied) Plover 22

Hawksbill Turtle 52
Heller's Scalesia 84
Hill Raspberry 82
Hoary Bat 40
Holy Stick 70

Isabela Snake 54

Jerusalem Thorn 72

Large Tree Finch 34
Large Ground Finch 32
Large Fernandina Mouse 40
Large Cactus Finch 32
Lava Cactus 70
Lava Heron 14
Lava Gull 10
Leach's Storm Petrel 4
Least Sandpiper 18
Leatherleaf 70
Lepidodactylus lugrubris 58
Longhaired Scalesia 84

Madeiran (Band-rumped) Storm
   Petrel 4
Magnificent Frigatebird 8
Maiden fern 86
Mangrove Finch 34
Marine Iguana 60
Medium Tree Finch 34
Medium Ground Finch 32
Minke Whale 46
Moorhen (Common Gallinule) 26

Narrowleaf Midsorus fern 86
Nazca Booby 6

Orca (Killer Whale) 48
Osprey 24

Paint-billed Crake 26
Passion Flower 74
Peregrine Falcon 24
Phyllodactylus reissi 58
Pink Land Iguana 60
Piscidia 70
Poison Apple 72
Polypodium tridens 86
Prickly Pear Cactus 70
Purple Martin 28

Quinine Tree 82

Radiate-headed Scalesia 84
Red Mangrove 64
Red-billed Tropicbird 6
Red-footed Booby 6
Red-necked Phalarope 18
Risso's Dolphin 48
Rock Pigeon 26
Royal Tern 10
Ruddy Turnstone 22

Saltbush 66
Saltwort 66
San Cristóbal Mockingbird 30
San Cristóbal Lava Lizard 56
Sanderling 22

Santa Fé Land Iguana 60
Santiago Mouse 40
Scalesia atractyloides 84
Sea Grape 66
Sei Whale 46
Semipalmated Plover 22
Sharp-beaked Ground Finch 32
Shieldhead Gecko 58
Short-beaked Common Dolphin
    48
Short-eared Owl 24
Short-finned Pilot Whale 48
Small Tree Finch 34
Small Ground Finch 32
Small Fernandina Mouse 40
Smooth-billed Ani 26
Snowy Egret 14
Sooty Shearwater 4
Sooty Tern 10
Sperm Whale 46
Spiny-headed Chaff Flower 76
Spotted Sandpiper 22
St. George's Milkwort 66
Steindachner's Snake 54
Stewart's Scalesia 84
Striated Heron 14
Surfbird 22
Swallow-tailed Gull 10

Thin-leafed Darwin's Shrub 74
Thorn Shrub 74
Thread-leafed Chaff Flower 76
Tiquilia 76
Toothed Sword Fern 86
Tree Scalesia 80

Vegetarian Finch 34
Vermilion Flycatcher 28

Waltheria 74
Wandering Tattler 18
Warbler Finch 34
Waved Albatross 2
Whimbrel 18
White mangrove 64
White-cheeked (Galápagos)
    Pintail 16
White-haired Tournefortia 74
Willett 18
Wilson's Phalarope 18
Wing-fruited Lecocarpus 76
Woodpecker Finch 34

Yellow Warbler 28
Yellow Cordia 72
Yellow-crowned Night Heron 14

VERZEICHNIS

Adlerfarn 82
Akazie 72
Alternanthera 76
Amerikanischer Sandregenpfeifer 22
Amerikanischer Graureiher 14

Balsambaum 70
Bärlapp 82
Bindenfregattvogel 8
Blauflügelente 16
Blaufußtölpel 6
Blauwal 46
Braunmantel-Austernfischer 16
Braunpelikan 8
Brombeere 82
Brydewal 46
Buckelwal 46

Chamaesyce 76
Chinarindenbaum 82
Cuvier-Schnabelwal 48

Darwiniothamnus 74
Dickschnabel-Darwinfink 34
Drosseluferläufer 22

Echte Karettschildkröte 52
Eisgraue Fledermaus 40
Española-Spottdrossel 30
Española-Lavaechse 56
Española-Schlange 54

Felsentaube 26
Fischadler 24
Flammenbaum 72
Floreana-Spottdrossel 30
Floreana-Lecocarpus 76
Floreana-Schlange 54
Franklin-Möwe 10

Gabelschwanzmöwe 10

Galápagos-Ralle 26
Galápagos-Spottdrossel 30
Galápagos-Schopftyrann 28
Galápagos-Bahamaente 16
Galápagos-Baumfarn 82
Galápagos-Baumwolle 74
Galápagos-Blattfingergecko 58
Galápagos-Bromelie 80
Galápagos-Bussard 24
Galápagos-Castela 76
Galápagos-Croton 72
Galápagos-Feigenkaktus 70
Galápagos-Fledermaus 40
Galápagos-Guave 80
Galápagos-Lavaechse 56
Galápagos-Lavakaktus 70
Galápagos-Miconia 82
Galápagos-Mistel 80
Galápagos-Nolana 66
Galápagos-Polygala 66
Galápagos-Portulak 66
Galápagos-Reisratte 40
Galápagos-Riesenschildkröte 52
Galápagos-Robbe 44
Galápagos-Säulenkaktus 70
Galápagos-Schleiereule 24
Galápagos-Schwalbe 28
Galápagos-Seebär 44
Galápagos-Seelöwe 44
Galápagos-Sesuvie 66
Galápagos-Sumpfohreule 24
Galápagos-Taube 26
Galápagos-Tomate 74
Galápagos-Wandelröschen 76
Galapagosalbatros 2
Galápagosbraunpelikan 8
Galápagosflamingo 16
Galápagoskormoran 8
Galapagospinguin 2
Galápagossturmtaucher 2
Gelbe Cordie 72
Gemeiner 48

Gischtläufer 22
Glattschnabel ani 26
Goldschnabel-Sumpfhuhn 26
Goldwaldsänger 28
Gonatodes caudiscutatus 58
Großer Rippenfarn 86
Große Fernandina-Maus 40
Großer Baumfink 34
Großer Schwertwal 48
Großer Tümmler 48
Großer Kaktusfink 32
Großer Grundfink 32
Grüne Meeresschildkröte 52

Isabela-Schlange 54

Kaffee 80
Kaktus-G rundfink 32
Kiebitzregenpfeifer 22
Kleine Fernandina-Maus 40
Kleiner Grundfink 32
Kleiner Rippenfarn 86
Kleiner Schwertwal 48
Kleiner Baumfink 34
Knopfmangrove 64
Königsseeschwalbe 10
Kuhreiher 14
Kurzflossen-Grindwal 48

Landleguan 60
Lavamöwe 10
Lavareiher 14
Lepidodactylus lugrubri 58

Mancinellenbaum 72
Mangrovenfink 34
Mangrovenreiher 14
Matazarno 70
Maytenus 70
Meerechse 60
Mittlerer Baumfink 34
Mittlerer Grundfink 32

Nachtreiher 14
Nazcatölpel 6
Noddi-Seeschwalbe 10
Nördlicher Zwergwal 46

Odinshühnchen 18
Orca 48

Parkinsonie 72
Passionsblume 74
Peruanischer Blattfingergecko 58
Phyllodactlyus bauri 58
Polypodium tridens 86
Pottwal 46
Prachtfregattvogel 8
Purpurschwalbe 28

Rauchschwalbe 28
Regenbrachvogel 18
Regenkuckuck 26
Reisstärling 30
Rosafarbener Landleguan 60
Rote Mangrove 64
Rotfußtölpel 6

Rotschnabel-Tropikvogel 6
Rubintyrann 28
Rundkopfdelfin 48
Rußseeschwalbe 10

Salzbusch 66
Salzkraut 66
San Cristóbal-Spottdrossel 30
San Cristóbal-Lavaechse 56
Sanderling 22
Santa Fé-Landleguan 60
Scaevola 66
Scalesia crockeri 84
Scalesia stewartii 84
Scalesia affinis 84
Scalesia atractyloides 84
Scalesia helleri 84
Scalesia villosa 84
Schlammtreter 18
Schmuckreiher 14
Schwarze Mangrove 64
Schwarznacken-Stelzenläufer 18
Schwertfarn 86
Scutia 74

Segge 76
Seiwal 46
Silberreiher 14
Sonnenblumenbaum 80
Spechtfink 34
Spitzschnabel-Grundfink 32
Steindachner-Schlange 54
Steinwälzer 22
Strandwinde 66
Sumpffarn 86

Teichhuhn 26
Tiquilia 76
Tournefortia pubescens 74
Waldsängerfink 34
Waltheria 74
Wanderfalke 24
Wanderwasserläufer 18
Weiße Mangrove 64
Wiesenstrandläufer 22
Wilsonwassertreter 18
Wurmfarn 86

LOS NOMBRES CIENTÍFICOS

SCIENTIFIC NAMES

WISSENSCHAFTLICHE BEZEICHNUNGEN

Acacia spp. 72
Actitis macularius 22
Aegialomys galapagoensis 40
Alsophis dorsalis 54
Alsophis steindachneri 54
Alsophis hoodensis 54
Altenanthera echinocephala 76
Alternanthera filifolia 76
Amblyrhynchus cristatus 60
Anas discors 16
Anas bahamensis galapapagensis 16
Anous stolidus galapagensis10
Aphriza virgata 22
Arctocephalus galapagoensis 44
Ardea herodias cognata 14
Arenaria interpres 22
Avicennia germinans 64

Balaenoptera edeni 46
Balaenoptera musculus 46
Balaenoptera acutrostrata 46
Balaenoptera borealis 46
Batis maritima 66
Blechnum occidentale 86
Blechnum polypodioides 86
Brachycereus nesioticus 70
Bubulcus ibis 14
Bursera graveolens 70
Buteo galapagoensis 24
Butorides sundevalli 14
Butorides striata 14

Calidris alba 22
Calidris minutilla 22
Camarhynchus pallidus 34

Camarhynchus parvulus 34
Camarhynchus heliobates 34
Camarhynchus psittacula 34
Camarhynchus pauper 34
Casmerodius albus 14
Castela galapageia 76
Catoptrophorus semipalmatus 18
Certhidea olivacea 34
Chamaesyce amplexicaulis 76
Charadrius semipalmatus 22
Chelonia mydas agassizi 52
Chelonoidis nigra 52
Cinchona succirubra 82
Coccyzus melacoryphus 26
Coffea arabica 80
Columba livia 26
Conocarpus erectus 64
Conolophus pallidus 60
Conolophus subcristatus 60
Conolophus marthae 60
Cordia lutea 72
Creagrus furcatus 10
Croton scouleri 72
Crotophaga ani 26
Cryptocarpus pyriformis 66
Ctenitis sloanei 86
Cyathea weatherbyana 82
Cyperus andersonii 76

Darwiniothamnus tenuifolius 74
Delonix regia 72
Delphinus delphis 48
Dendroica petechia 28
Dolichonyx oryzivorus 30

Egretta thula 14

Epidendrum spicatum 80
Eretmochelys imbricata 52

Falco peregrinus 24
Fregata m. magnificens 8
Fregata minor 8

Gallinula chloropus 26
Geospiza conirostris 32
Geospiza difficilis 32
Geospiza fuliginosa 32
Geospiza fortis 32
Geospiza magnirostris 32
Geospiza scandens 32
Globicephala macrorhyncus 48
Gonatodes caudiscutatus 58
Gossypium darwinii 74
Grampus grisius 48

Haematopus palliatus 16
Heteroscelus incanus 18
Himantopus mexicanus 18
Hippomane mancinella 72
Hirundo rustica 28

Ipomoea pes-caprae 66

Jasminocereus thouarsii 70

Laguncularia racemosa 64
Lantana peduncularis 76
Larus pipixcan 10
Larus fuliginosus 10
Lasiurus cinereus 40
Lasiurus borealis brachyotis 40
Laterallus spilonotus 26

Lecocarpus pinnatifidus 76
Lepidodactylus lugrubris 58
Licopodium cernuum 82

Maytenus octogona 70
Megaptera novaeangliae 46
Miconia robinsoniana 82
Mimus macdonaldi 30
Mimus melanotis 30
Mimus trifasciatus 30
Mimus parvulus 30
Myiarchus magnirostris 28

Neocrex erythrops 26
Nephrolepis pectinata 86
Nesoryzomys fernandinae 40
Nesoryzomys narboroughi 40
Nesoryzomys swarthi 40
Nolana galapagensis 66
Numenius phaeopus 18
Nyctanassa violaceus pauper 14

Oceanites gracilis galapagoensis 4
Oceanodroma tethys tethys 4
Oceanodroma castro 4
Oceanodroma leucorhoa 4
Opuntia spp. 70
Orcinus orca 48

Pandion haliaetus 24
Parkinsonia aculeata 72
Passiflora suberosa 74
Pelecanus occidentalis urinator 8

Phaethon aethereus 6
Phalacrocorax harrisi 8
Phalaropus lobatus 18
Phoebastria irrorata 2
Phoenicopterus ruber
  glyphorhynchus16
Phoradendron henslowii 80
Phyllodactylus reissi 58
Phyllodactylus bauri 58
Phyllodactylus galapagoensis 58
Physeter macrocephalus 46
Piscidia carthagenensis 70
Platyspiza crassirostris 34
Pluvialis squatarola 22
Polygala sancti-georgii 66
Polypodium tridens 86
Portulaca howellii 66
Progne modesta 28
Progne subis 28
Pseudorca crassidens 48
Psidium galapageium 80
Pteridium aquilinum 82
Pterodroma phaeopygia 4
Puffinus subalaris 2
Puffinus griseus 4
Pyrocephalus rubinus 28

Racinaea insularis 80
Rhizophora mangle 64
Rubus niveus 82

Scaevola plumieri 66
Scalesia helleri 84

Scalesia crockeri 84
Scalesia villosa 84
Scalesia stewartii 84
Scalesia atractyloides 84
Scalesia affinis 84
Scalesia pedunculata 80
Scutia spicata 74
Sesuvium edmonstonei 66
Solanum cheesmaniae 74
Spheniscus mendiculus 2
Steganopus tricolor 18
Sterna maxima 10
Sterna fuscata 10
Sula sula websteri 6
Sula nebouxii excisa 6
Sula granti 6

Thelypteris oligocarpa 86
Tiquilia nesiotica 76
Tournefortia pubescens 74
Tropidurus delanonis 56
Tropidurus bivattatus 56
Tropidurus albemarlensis 56
Tursiops truncatus 48
Tyto alba punctatissima 24

Waltheria ovata 74

Zalophus wollebaeki 44
Zenaida galapagoensis 26
Ziphius cavirostris 48